100 THINGS TO DO IN AUBURN, AL BEFORE YOU DIE

Samford Hall iconic symbol of Auburn since 1859.

100 THINGS TO DO IN AUBURN, AL BEFORE YOU DIE

CONNIE PEARSON

Copyright © 2023 by Reedy Press, LLC
Reedy Press
PO Box 5131
St. Louis, MO 63139, USA
www.reedypress.com

No part of this publication may be reproduced or transmitted in any form or by any means, electronic or mechanical, including photocopy, recording, or any information storage and retrieval system, without permission in writing from the publisher.

Permissions may be sought directly from Reedy Press at the above mailing address or via our website at www.reedypress.com.

Library of Congress Control Number: 2023935947

ISBN: 9781681064512

Design by Jill Halpin

All photos are by the author unless otherwise noted.

Printed in the United States of America
26 27   5 4 3 2

We (the publisher and the author) have done our best to provide the most accurate information available when this book was completed. However, we make no warranty, guarantee, or promise about the accuracy, completeness, or currency of the information provided, and we expressly disclaim all warranties, express or implied. Please note that attractions, company names, addresses, websites, and phone numbers are subject to change or closure, and this is outside of our control. We are not responsible for any loss, damage, injury, or inconvenience that may occur due to the use of this book. When exploring new destinations, please do your homework before you go. You are responsible for your own safety and health when using this book.

DEDICATION

To my husband Steve, a 1972 graduate of the Auburn University School of Veterinary Medicine, who was quick to share his devotion to Auburn the first time we met.

And to the many members of the Pearson family, past and present, who are proud of their Auburn degrees and look great in orange and blue: Grandaddy Elton Pearson, brother and sister-in-law David and Susie Pearson, niece Jenny Pearson Herman, niece Becky Collier, nephew Jon David Pearson and his wife Tucker, daughter and son-in-law David and Laura (Pearson) Baggett, son and daughter-in-law Matt and Katie Pearson.

Matt, Julie, and Laura, I hope you'll forgive your dad and me for telling you that Santa Claus wouldn't come if you said "R_____ T_____." But I'm so glad you learned to say "WAR EAGLE" when you were very small.

CONTENTS

Foreword .... **xii**

Acknowledgments .... **xiii**

Food and Drink

1. Taste Why Chef David Bancroft Is One of the South's Best by Dining at Acre **2**

2. Discover Amsterdam Café, A Gem on Gay Street **3**

3. Have an Authentic Italian Meal at Ariccia Cucina **4**

4. Experience World-Class Service and Cuisine at 1856 Culinary Residence **6**

5. Make a Special Occasion Even More Delightful at Café 123 .... **8**

6. Come As You Are for Lunch or Dinner at Hamilton's on Magnolia **9**

7. Imagine Scenes from the 1800s during a Fine Meal at the Depot **10**

8. Admire the Furnishings While You Eat a Great Meal at the Hound **12**

9. Refresh with Lemonade at Toomer's Drugs **14**

10. Take Your Own Good Vibes into Lucy's **15**

11. Join the Movement and the Line at the Irritable Bao **16**

12. Feast on Gulf Seafood, Wild Game, and More at Vintage 2298 .... **17**

13. Shop, Stroll the Grounds, and Dine at Botanic **18**

14. Chow Down with Other Proud Auburn Fans at Niffer's Place **20**

15. Make the Drive to Find Relaxation and Great Food at the Waverly Local **21**

16. Sink Your Teeth Into a Signature Sandwich at Momma Goldberg's Deli **22**

17. Eat a Piece of History at Guthrie's in Auburn **23**

18. Appreciate the Longevity and Great Food at Country's Barbecue... **24**

19. Step Up to the Window at Mrs. Story's Dairy Bar **25**

20. Devour a Great Steak or Fresh Oysters at Big Mike's Steakhouse... **26**

21. Choose Chipped or Chopped Pork at Chuck's Bar-B-Que **27**

22. Dine Sumptuously in Vintage Surroundings at Zazu Gastropub..... **28**

23. Taste Slow-Smoked, Texas-Style Barbecue at Bow & Arrow **30**

24. Eat Breakfast with the Locals at Byron's Smokehouse **31**

25. Get Your Morning Java and a Sugar Rush at Mo'Bay Beignet Co. **32**

26. Check Out One of Bo Jackson's Favorites at Pannie-George's Kitchen **34**

27. Try an Ethnic Dish at Hey Day Market **35**

28. Satisfy Your Curiosity about Korean Cuisine at Chickchickporkpork **36**

29. Request a Spot on the Patio at LiveOaks **38**

30. Be Transported to Ireland at Irish Bred Pub **39**

31. Celebrate Your Birthday with a Free Dinner at Venditori's **40**

32. Savor Favorites from Bayou Country at Walk-On's Sports Bistreaux **41**

33. Taste Homemade Flavor at Sheila C's Burger Barn **42**

Music and Entertainment

34. Be Dazzled by the Talent at the Jay and Susie Gogue Performing Arts Center **46**

35. Discover a Rising Star at the Opelika Songwriters Festival and the Sound Wall **47**

36. Join the Crowd for Oktoberfest at Ag Heritage Park **48**

37. Sample, Shop, and Listen at On the Tracks—A Wine and Cheese Event **49**

38. Watch the Bull Riders or Dance to the Music at Auburn Rodeo **50**

39. Get a Closeup Look at Raptors during "Football, Fans, and Feathers" **51**

40. Pitch a Tent for Tailgating before Home Football Games **52**

41. Buy a Ticket for a Performance at the Opelika Center for the Performing Arts **54**

42. Try Out for a Part at Auburn Area Community Theatre **55**

43. Listen to Country Music at Old 280 Boogie at Standard Deluxe in Waverly **56**

44. Peek Inside Beautiful Buildings During the Loveliest Village Christmas Tour **57**

45. Find Original Crafts at Syrup Soppin' Day in Pioneer Park at Loachapoka **58**

46. Admire the Gingerbread Village Inside the Hotel at Auburn University **60**

47. Step Back in Time at a Victorian Front Porch Christmas Tour **62**

48. Catch Beads at the Mardi Gras Parade in Downtown Auburn **64**

49. Find a Spot at Monkey Park for the Summer Swing Concert Series **66**

50. Head to Kiesel Park in the Spring for Auburn CityFest **67**

Sports and Recreation

51. Surround Yourself with Nature at Kreher Preserve and Nature Center **70**

52. Solve the Mysteries at Auburn Escape Zones **71**

53. Go Mountain Biking or Camping at Chewacla State Park **72**

54. Hit the Target at Tumble Tree Disc Golf **74**

55. Learn to Play a Popular New Sport at the Opelika Pickleball Facility **75**

56. Bring Your Binoculars to One of the Piedmont Plateau Birding Trails **76**

57. Escape the Rain and Cold with Indoor Fun at Good Times Bowling **77**

58. Improve Your Aim at the Opelika Community Archery Park **78**

59. Grab Some Friends and Head to Tigertown Sports **79**

60. Sink a Putt at Grand National Golf Course in Opelika **80**

61. Drive the Auburn Floral Trail in the Spring **81**

62. Cast Your Rod and Catch your Supper at Lee County Public Fishing Lake **82**

63. Improve Your Backhand at Yarbrough Tennis Center **83**

64. Watch the Eagle Soar at Jordan-Hare Stadium **84**

65. Add Your Rumble to the Jungle at Neville Arena **85**

66. Join the Throng for Tiger Walk before Home Football Games **86**

67. Catch a Homerun Ball at Plainsman Park (Samford Stadium–Hitchcock Field) **88**

68. Test Your Inner Daredevil Skills at the New Auburn–Opelika Skate Park **89**

69. Roll Toomer's Corner after a Big Auburn Victory **90**

70. Support a Great Cause by Biking in Bo Bikes Bama **91**

71. Zipline Across the Alabama/Georgia State Line **92**

Culture and History

72. Learn Surprising History at the Museum of East Alabama **96**

73. Watch for Ghosts at Salem-Shotwell Covered Bridge **97**

74. Recall Great Auburn Athletes as You Walk the Tiger Trail **98**

75. Marvel at Intricate Specimens Inside the Museum of Natural History **100**

76. Watch Auburn Theatre Students Perform at the Telfair B. Peet Theatre **101**

77. Tour the Jule Collins Smith Museum of Fine Art **102**

78. Find the 11 Public Murals in Auburn and Opelika **104**

79. Be Surprised at the Museum of Wonder in Seale **105**

80. Dig Deeper into African American History at Nearby Tuskegee University **106**

81. Take a Class and See Works by Local Artists at Art Haus **108**

82. Visit Pebble Hill and Learn of its Ties to the Civil War and Auburn **110**

Shopping and Fashion

83. Find Vintage and New Vinyl Records at 10,000 Hz Records **114**

84. Spend Hours Searching for Treasures at Angel's Antique & Flea Mall **115**

85. Buy Everything Orange and Blue at the Auburn University Bookstore **116**

86. Choose the Perfect Touch for Your Home at Artifactory **118**

87. Show Your Loyalty to Auburn with Items from Auburn Art **119**

88. Carry On a Long-Standing Tradition by Visiting J & M Bookstore **120**

89. Make Your Special Someone Smile with a Gift from Ware Jewelers **122**

90. Gather, Read, and Sample Treats at Well Red Coffee, Books & Wine **123**

91. Add Style to Your Wardrobe at Behind the Glass **124**

92. Entertain and Decorate Glamorously with Help from the Gallery on Railroad.. **125**

93. Enjoy Browsing in an Elegant Setting at Wakefield Home **126**

94. Walk Out with a Beautifully Wrapped Package at Southern Crossing **127**

95. See the Results of a Mother-Daughter Effort at Fig & Wasp in Waverly... **128**

96. Buy Gifts with Meaning at Wrapsody in Downtown Auburn......... **129**

97. Meet Friends and Read a Great Book at Auburn Oil Co. Booksellers **130**

98. Create a Signature Scent at Auburn Candle Company.................... **131**

99. Find the Perfect Slouchy and More at the Mint Julep Boutique...... **132**

100. Buy an Aubie Cookie or an Architecturally Stunning Cake at Cakeitecture **134**

Activities by Season **137**

Suggested Itineraries **140**

Index **143**

FOREWORD

The Auburn Creed was written in 1943 by George Petrie. Students are encouraged to memorize it, and framed copies grace the homes and offices of many Auburn alumni.

I believe that this is a practical world and that I can count only on what I earn. Therefore, I believe in work, hard work.

I believe in education, which gives me the knowledge to work wisely and trains my mind and my hands to work skillfully.

I believe in honesty and truthfulness, without which I cannot win the respect and confidence of my fellow men.

I believe in a sound mind, in a sound body and a spirit that is not afraid, and in clean sports that develop these qualities.

I believe in obedience to law because it protects the rights of all.

I believe in the human touch, which cultivates sympathy with my fellow men and mutual helpfulness and brings happiness for all.

I believe in my Country, because it is a land of freedom and because it is my own home, and that I can best serve that country by "doing justly, loving mercy, and walking humbly with my God."

And because Auburn men and women believe in these things, I believe in Auburn and love it.

ACKNOWLEDGMENTS

Much gratitude for help with this project goes to my long-time friend Talitha Culver who has been an Auburn resident for many years and to Robyn Bridges, President of Auburn-Opelika Tourism. Both provided insightful advice and direction, as well as much-appreciated encouragement.

Dessert at 1856 Culinary Residence

FOOD AND DRINK

1

TASTE WHY CHEF DAVID BANCROFT IS ONE OF THE SOUTH'S BEST

BY DINING AT ACRE

Acre is a restaurant whose list of awards continues to grow. The location is a short two-block walk from Toomer's Corner, a spot almost sacred to the Auburn faithful. The building and one-acre lot are beautifully designed with great architecture and landscaping filled with fruit trees, herbs, and vegetable plants. The passionate owner and chef, David Bancroft, is skilled, creative, and consistently nominated by the James Beard Foundation as one of the best chefs in the South. A reservation for dinner at Acre is coveted indeed.

Chef Bancroft is committed to locally sourced produce and meats and the best seafood from the Alabama Gulf Coast. Bancroft works with the Auburn University Meat Lab and local ranchers to serve responsibly farm-raised meat at Acre. The menu changes seasonally to maximize the local fresh ingredients. Dishes reflect the Deep South with innovative, modern twists. Acre is open for dinner Monday through Saturday, for lunch Wednesday through Saturday, and for brunch on Sunday.

210 E Glenn Ave., 334-246-3763
acreauburn.com

2

DISCOVER AMSTERDAM CAFÉ

A GEM ON GAY STREET

Amsterdam Café has been a fixture on South Gay Street since 1991. Its intimate interior spills out onto the patio. A favorite feature is the Van Gogh theme and artwork inside, which gives it a very distinctive look.

The menu is small, but entrée prices range from affordable to pricey, making this a student-budget-friendly eatery as well as a place to splurge on prime filet mignon. Seafood is prominent on the menu, with lobster egg rolls, calamari, grouper, scallops, shrimp, and tuna, but there are non-seafood options as well. Cookie dough egg rolls are available for dessert along with three cakes. Amsterdam Café is open for dinner Monday through Saturday and for brunch on Sunday.

The Dam Food Truck and The Dam Taco Truck can often be found on the university campus, making it possible for students to grab quick sandwiches, wraps, burgers, tacos, or chicken fingers. A second café called Amsterdam in the Park recently opened in Auburn Research Park.

410 S Gay St., 334-826-8181
amsterdamcafe.com

3

HAVE AN AUTHENTIC ITALIAN MEAL

AT ARICCIA CUCINA

Ariccia Cucina is an exceptional Italian restaurant located inside one of Auburn's most recognizable and centrally located hotels. Wood-fired pizzas and homemade focaccia are favorites, and the Porchetta de Ariccia (slow-roasted pork) recently made the list of "100 Dishes to Eat in Alabama." Pasta is made and cut in-house daily, and Pastry Chef Dallas Kee produces swoonworthy affogato, gelato, cheesecake, and fried zeppolis.

The atmosphere is magical, with hedges, a pergola draped in twinkling lights, and the splashing sounds of a large fountain. Ariccia opened in 2001 and is named for the town that hosts an Auburn Abroad program in Italy. The partnership with that campus has contributed to incredible meats and cheeses and a wine cellar boasting 1,500 bottles. Ariccia Cucina serves brunch daily, and tomatoes grown in Auburn greenhouses enhance many of the dishes. Piccolo, the area's only true jazz lounge, is adjacent to Ariccia Cucina, and the two partner in offering wine dinners and musical performances for their guests.

241 S College St., 334-844-5140
aricciacucina.com

The Hotel at Auburn University is a AAA Four Diamond property boasting 235 guestrooms and suites a block from Toomer's Corner and across the street from Ralph Brown Draughon Library.

241 S College St., 334-821-8200
auhcc.com

4

EXPERIENCE WORLD-CLASS SERVICE AND CUISINE

AT 1856 CULINARY RESIDENCE

The Tony and Libba Rane Culinary Science Center opened in the fall of 2022 and is raking in the superlatives. The showplace teaching restaurant inside is 1856 Culinary Residence, referring to the year Auburn was founded. Every year the school will have a chef-in-residence, teaching the students and offering highly elevated dining experiences for the guests.

Dinner offerings consist of a seven- to nine-course tasting menu for prix fixe, while lunch is more casual and a la carte. The open kitchen concept allows you to watch the culinary staff at work, and the dining room has soaring ceilings with floor-to-ceiling windows. A two-story wine room is a stunning feature.

For lunch, I can personally vouch for the Tarte Flambee, the Fried Fish Sandwich, and the Yuzu Meringue Tart. The presentation for every dish is artistic and thoughtfully planned. Be sure to visit the Rooftop Terrace, where herbs, flowers, and vegetables are planted to be used in the restaurant's dishes.

Corner of College Street and Thach Avenue
205 S College St., Auburn
ranecenter.auburn.edu
auburn1856.com

The Laurel Hotel and Spa is included in the hospitality degree program at Auburn. Expect the highest quality amenities and level of attention when you book a room at the Laurel or a treatment at the spa.

130 E Thach Ave., 833-950-1819
laurelhotelandspa.com

MAKE A SPECIAL OCCASION EVEN MORE DELIGHTFUL

AT CAFÉ 123

Café 123 is an intimate, fine dining restaurant offering a small menu of classic Southern dishes with a French flair. Reservations are taken via phone only. Dinner is served Tuesday through Saturday, and brunch is offered on weekends.

Executive Chef and General Manager Eron Bass is a lifelong resident of Opelika, who learned a lot about cooking from watching both of his grandmothers and his parents. Café 123 is in the former Haynie's Drugstore building, and the original walnut cabinets are still in place. Tables are adorned with white tablecloths and soft candlelight.

Brown Sugar Rub Ribeye is made with a signature rub created by Chef Bass that caramelizes on the steak. The classic tableside Caesar salad for two is a great way to begin your meal. Other favorites are the Blackened Redfish and the Grilled Shrimp and Crispy Fried Grits. Café 123 is a great spot for a special occasion.

123 S 8th St., Opelika, 334-737-0069
cafeonetwentythree.com

6

COME AS YOU ARE FOR LUNCH OR DINNER

AT HAMILTON'S ON MAGNOLIA

Hamilton's on Magnolia has a "come one, come all" neighborhood atmosphere. Co-owner George Spence even says with a twinkle in his eye, "We want everyone to come in and feel welcome, even if they're an Alabama fan." On any given day you'll see students in shorts sitting at tables near men in three-piece suits.

The cuisine is described as casual fine dining. Shrimp & Grits is made extra special with cheese in the grits and Capps Sausage from nearby Opelika, Alabama, while the Fried Green Tomatoes are elevated with the addition of grilled shrimp. Chocoholics will want to save room for the Chocolate Chip Bread Pudding or the Lava Cake. Owners and partners George and Regena Spence and Jim and Lisa Parker can't say enough good things about Chef Pat Gallagher, who has been at Hamilton's since 2000. In their opinion, any dish he creates is "the best in town." Hamilton's has expanded to a second location at 1849 Ogletree Road in Auburn.

174 E Magnolia Ave., 334-887-2677
magnolia.hamiltonsgroup.com

7

IMAGINE SCENES FROM THE 1800S

DURING A FINE MEAL AT THE DEPOT

The Depot is steeped in history while also serving outstanding meals. The important train depot was first built in 1847 but had to be rebuilt in 1870 because of destruction caused by Union troops known as "Rousseau's Raiders." Original elements of the depot have been woven into the present-day décor, such as the black and white tiles in the floors and the knotted pine in the bar and hostess stand.

You'll find steak, chicken, and pork dishes listed with the entrees, but seafood is more prominent. There are daily specials along with daily oyster selections. Eight sides with Southern roots and four dessert options round out the enticing menu. Executive Chef and owner Scott Simpson is proud that the Depot was the first in Alabama to receive the James Beard Smart Catch Leader Award for serving sustainable and responsibly harvested seafood. The Depot has also received the Wine Spectator Excellence Award for six years. the Depot serves dinner Tuesday through Saturday.

124 Mitcham Ave., 334-521-5177
allaboardauburn.com

TIP

The origin of the Wreck Tech Pajama Parade, called "the most comfortable college football tradition of all time," began at the Depot in November 1896. Ask for details when you are in town.

Speaking of seafood at the Depot, Auburn University's School of Fisheries, Aquaculture, and Aquatics is one of the best in thc world. Schedule tours of the E. W. Shell Fisheries Center by contacting David Cline at clinedj@auburn.edu.

2101 N College St., 334-844-4667
agriculture.auburn.edu/%20research/faas/e-w-shell-fisheries-center

8

ADMIRE THE FURNISHINGS

WHILE YOU EAT A GREAT MEAL AT THE HOUND

Matt and Jana (Caruthers) Poirier opened their restaurant on Tichenor Avenue in March 2012. Matt is from California, but Jana and members of her immediate family are Auburn alums. The décor is a blend of rustic, reclaimed wood, with a hunting theme represented by mounted game skulls. You'll find hand-crafted doors and furniture created by skilled family members and antler chandeliers.

"Bacon & Bourbon" is so integral to the Hound's culinary experience that it is part of the name. Executive Chef Robbie Nicolaisen is a wizard with bacon creations, and the list of bourbons on the menu is extensive. Wild game options include duck wings, bison chili, and rabbit pappardelle. Especially popular dishes are shrimp and grits, the meatloaf, and the BTA sandwich on the lunch menu, which features bacon, smoked turkey, and avocado.

The Hound is open for brunch, lunch, and dinner throughout the week. You can make a reservation through the website EXCEPT during home football game weekends and Auburn graduation weekends.

124 Tichenor Ave., 334-246-3300
thehound-auburn.com

TIPS

The rocking chairs in the reception area of the Hound were made by SNF Outdoor Products in nearby Camp Hill, Alabama. Check out @snfoutdoors on Facebook to contact them or place an order.

....

Brunch at the Hound includes coffee drinks provided by Coffee Cat, the local coffee shop next door. Parking is available in the Auburn Bank parking deck located right outside the front door.

9

REFRESH WITH LEMONADE
AT TOOMER'S DRUGS

There's more to Toomer's Drugs than lemonade, but that fresh-squeezed fruity drink has drawn customers since 1896. Toomer's Lemonade may be purchased by the gallon jug if you're extra thirsty, and Aubie cookies infused with Toomer's Lemonade are a sought-after souvenir and treat. Soft drinks and ice cream cones can also be purchased inside along with Auburn-themed Game Day apparel in this former pharmacy with a nostalgic soda fountain.

Toomer's Drugs derives its name from founder Shel Toomer, whose Auburn ties run deep. He played on the school's first football team, earned degrees in pharmacy and agriculture, and represented Lee County in Alabama's House of Representatives. This iconic building on the corner of College Street and Magnolia Avenue has served as the official dividing line between the town of Auburn and the university campus, but that line has blurred increasingly over the years. The town and the university, which continue to grow in national recognition, fully embrace each other.

100 N College St., 334-887-3488
toomers.com

TIP

Parking is easy when you are in downtown Auburn. There are two large parking decks: one is at Auburn Bank, and the other is on Wright Street.

10

TAKE YOUR OWN GOOD VIBES

INTO LUCY'S

This visionary eatery designed by owner Lisa van der Reijden, is truly a neighborhood gathering spot. The tagline "Good Vibes Only" is fleshed out by the friendly staff, the stunning interior, and the creative and appealing menu. Some claim that Lucy's has the best weekend brunch in the area. The house roast coffee from nearby Mama Mocha's Coffee Roastery may be one of the reasons. House-made Coconut and Banana Toast and the Lemon Ricotta Hotcakes are brunch favorites.

Opened in 2018, Lucy's is one of the few places where you can enjoy dinner on Sunday evenings. In fact, Sunday nights are referred to as Neighborhood Nights, and the famous fried chicken is served until the supply runs out. Shareable plates, fresh oysters, and eight additional entrees, such as Shrimp and Green Chili Grits, are also features of the dinner menu. Chef Brian Paolina supports area farmers and artisans by incorporating their products into his dishes. Reservations are strongly encouraged.

2300 Moores Mill Rd., 334-521-0391
lucysauburn.com

11

JOIN THE MOVEMENT AND THE LINE

AT THE IRRITABLE BAO

Describing the Irritable Bao with its highly quirky name is somewhat difficult. Is this a cult following, a commitment to great causes, or just plain good food? Auburn students are now fans of its authentic and admittedly unusual Asian dishes, such as Bao and Chinese dumplings. The proof is in the long line that forms whenever the Irritable Bao is open. Food is packaged for carrying out, but there are tables available if you choose to sit and eat on the spot.

Owner Whitley Dykes grew up in Auburn but spent about eight years in China doing humanitarian work. While there, he met and fell in love with his wife, Kunyu Li. He also fell in love with the snowy-white, meat-filled steamed buns served in Li's home.

Dykes and his restaurant contribute to causes that feed, educate, and empower children around the world. Give the Irritable Bao a try. Join the Bao movement. The food is delicious!

127 W Magnolia St., 334-329-7009
facebook.com/foodtruckwithacause

12

FEAST ON GULF SEAFOOD, WILD GAME, AND MORE

AT VINTAGE 2298

Chef-owner Randall Baldwin has been strongly influenced by his mother throughout his life by her Southern, coastal cooking style and her encouragement to follow his passion and dreams. Although she died in 2004, her presence is woven throughout Vintage 2298, which opened in late 2022 and features a painting of her above the kitchen. She taught him to make biscuits when he was very young and showed him the secrets to frying fish and hushpuppies. Her name was Nancy, and you'll spot Nancy's Buttermilk Fried Chicken and Nancy's Pecan Pie as you peruse the menu's offerings.

Although the menu changes daily, it consistently features Alabama fish from the Gulf and wild game from the forests. Produce will often be picked from trellises right outside the kitchen. Vintage 2298 (with the name derived from the 2298 East University Drive address) is open for dinner on Monday and Wednesday through Saturday and for brunch on Sunday.

2298 E University Dr., 334-521-5128
facebook.com/vintage2298

13

SHOP, STROLL THE GROUNDS, AND DINE
AT BOTANIC

Botanic is a gleaming new star in the restaurant scene of Opelika. The entire campus is beautifully landscaped and includes a massive greenhouse, a nursery, garden center, a pond, two restaurants, an outdoor patio bar, and a market for pastries, jams, sauces, gifts, and carry-out items. They also offer lawn and maintenance care services.

The Grille is a dinner-only, reservation-only fine dining restaurant. The Garden is more casual and is situated under a retractable roof, allowing for careful weather and temperature control. Vegetables served in the restaurants are locally sourced and will also be grown in the on-site greenhouse.

Stacy Brown and her husband, King Braswell, are the owners and co-creators of this space that combines their passions for restaurants and horticulture. This is a place to visit that will satisfy more than your appetite for food. It will also awaken your appreciation of nature and growing things.

1702 Frederick Rd., Opelika, 334-748-9082
shopbotanic.com

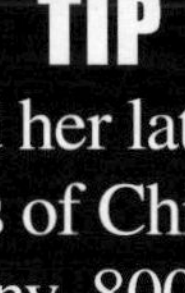

Stacy Brown and her late husband, Scott, were the founders of Chicken Salad Chick which started in a tiny, 800-square-foot takeout spot in Auburn in January 2008.

Chicken Salad Chick
1345 Opelika Rd., Ste. A, 334-459-9752
chickensaladchick.com/auburn-opelika

14

CHOW DOWN WITH OTHER PROUD AUBURN FANS

AT NIFFER'S PLACE

Niffer's Place was created by an Auburn person for Auburn people. Keely Beasecker, Auburn alumna and former swim team member, transformed a former Golden Corral restaurant in 1991 into a highly popular burger joint with no signs of slowing down. Niffer's is budget-friendly for students with nightly burger specials, and their corn nuggets with honey mustard dipping sauce are legendary.

You will find burgers and sandwiches on the menu with names such as The Sullivan (for Auburn's first Heisman trophy winner Pat Sullivan), The Orange & Blue (for the school colors), and The Bramlett (in memory of Rod Bramlett, who was the radio voice of the Auburn Tigers). The Cadillac, for superstar running back and interim head coach Cadillac Williams, is making the menu in 2023. House-made potato chips, homemade baked beans, and fried pickles are also very popular.

Niffer's has expanded beyond Auburn to Opelika and most recently to nearby Lake Martin. It is a must-visit for many Auburn fans.

1151 Opelika Rd., 334-821-3118
niffersplace.com/auburn
917 S Railroad Ave., Opelika, 334-787-5989
niffersplace.com/opelika
niffersplace.com/lake-martin

MAKE THE DRIVE TO FIND RELAXATION AND GREAT FOOD

AT THE WAVERLY LOCAL

If you're feeling a need to get away from the bustle of a large college campus and slow down for a bit, I suggest a drive out to the tiny town of Waverly. Patrick Street is the hub of Waverly, which gives a glimpse of the Deep South as it has been for several generations. The Waverly Local is a restaurant serving food that is well worth the extra time to find it. It is open for dinner Wednesday through Saturday evenings and for brunch on Sunday.

The menu is small, but if you want a steak, fish, chicken, pork, pasta, crab cakes, or a burger, you'll find it. The building housing the restaurant formerly served as one of the earliest Model T Ford dealerships in the State of Alabama. Chef Christian Watson changes the menu according to the seasons and availability of the freshest ingredients. You can look forward to specialty jams created exclusively for the Waverly Local by Hornsby Farms.

1465 Patrick St., Waverly, 334-539-6077
thewaverlylocal.com

16

SINK YOUR TEETH INTO A SIGNATURE SANDWICH

AT MOMMA GOLDBERG'S DELI

Momma Goldberg's Deli, located at the corner of South Magnolia Street and Donahue Drive, has been in business since 1976 and is the oldest independently owned restaurant in town. Don Dement started the business, but he has always been supported by members of his family, such as his wife Betty, brother Mike, and son Jason. His nephew Keith Schilleci was the first to open a separate Momma Goldberg's location on Thach Avenue. The W Magnolia Street restaurant is the most iconic, in part because of the clear view of Jordan-Hare Stadium from the front parking lot.

The Momma's Love sandwich, wrap, and salad are the signature items, and each contains three meats: roast beef, ham, and smoked turkey. The Build-Your-Own option is also popular. Diners may select from 10 breads, 11 meats, and 6 types of cheese. The menu is very simple, with a selection of sandwiches, wraps, salads, soups, and nachos. The prices are reasonable, which makes it very student friendly.

500 W Magnolia Ave., 334-821-0185
mommagoldbergsdeli.com

17

EAT A PIECE OF HISTORY
AT GUTHRIE'S IN AUBURN

Hal Guthrie, 1962 Auburn graduate, opened his first restaurant in Haleyville, Alabama, with a full menu of hamburger steaks, a salad bar, and Southern favorites. In 1982, he moved his business to Auburn. The new location was a renovated Sonic building with a tiny kitchen, so they brought only a fraction of the menu with them. At first, Guthrie's only served hamburgers, steak sandwiches, and chicken fingers, which were new on the culinary scene. Chicken fingers quickly began outselling the other items. In August 1982, the executive decision was made to serve only chicken fingers, which meant that Auburn was the home of the world's first chicken finger restaurant.

The successful but tiny menu is simple at Guthrie's: chicken fingers, French fries, coleslaw, Texas toast, sauce, and sweet tea. You can order chicken fingers in a box, on a bun, or in a family pack, but you'll get the same thing. Copycats are everywhere, but the Guthrie family knows they were first.

804 E Glenn Ave., 334-209-2233
guthrieschicken.com

APPRECIATE THE LONGEVITY AND GREAT FOOD

AT COUNTRY'S BARBECUE

Country's Barbecue in Auburn has been serving great food since 1975. All the barbecue is cooked over hickory and oak wood, and the Brunswick stew takes two full days of simmering to be just right. Pies are baked on-site, lemons are squeezed for the lemonade and lemon pie, and salad fixings and French fries are hand cut. To add to the ambiance, the Auburn location has live bluegrass music on Friday and Saturday nights.

In addition to barbecue platters, plates, and sandwiches, Country's Barbecue offers sides you might not find elsewhere. Skillet apples, barbecue onions, butter beans, and squash casserole are just a few. In the dessert section, you'll find root beer floats, goober pie, and banana pudding served in a pint jar. An intriguing beverage is the Arnold Palmer, which is half iced tea and half lemonade. Be sure to pose for a photo sitting in the big red rocking chair.

1021 Opelika Rd., 334-821-8711
auburncountrys.com

STEP UP TO THE WINDOW
AT MRS. STORY'S DAIRY BAR

Be very careful turning into Mrs. Story's Dairy Bar on Pepperell Parkway. The eatery is sometimes hard to spot, and the small parking lot will be crowded. Awesome hot dogs and milkshakes have been served here since 1952. The prices are great, and the taste is greater. Mrs. Story's Dairy Bar was forced to close in the fall of 2021. When it was able to reopen in late 2022, faithful customers breathed a sigh of relief and joined the lines to satisfy their cravings.

At Mrs. Story's, there is no inside seating. This is a stand-in-line-outside-in-all-kinds-of-weather type of place where you walk up to a window, place your order, and wait. Some eat in their cars, while others take their meals back home or to work to devour them. You can expect to find it open Monday through Saturday for lunch and early dinner. Find it soon for a homemade chili dog and a chocolate shake.

1900 Pepperell Pkwy., Opelika, 334-749-1719

DEVOUR A GREAT STEAK OR FRESH OYSTERS

AT BIG MIKE'S STEAKHOUSE

Three friends, Mike Cole, Scott Powell, and Caine Conway, shared a vision for opening quality steakhouses in rural towns, so that the residents would not have to drive for miles for a great meal. Their first restaurant opened in Thomasville. The great success there led to the idea of franchising, and the Auburn restaurant is now the fifth Big Mike's in Alabama.

Mike's serves amazing steaks from Angus beef that has been aged for 28 days and then hand cut, but the menu also includes chicken, fish, burgers, and pork. One eye-catching entrée is called Sweet Water Stack and consists of fried green tomatoes, crabcakes, shrimp, and remoulade sauce. Oysters are featured prominently and can be ordered on the half shell, chargrilled, Bienville, Rockefeller, or with Asian sauce, pickled jalapenos, and ghost pepper cheese. Cakes, bread pudding, and cheesecake are the dessert offerings, and onion straws are a popular appetizer.

610 Shug Jordan Pkwy., 334-209-1975
bigmikessteakhouse.com/auburn

21

CHOOSE CHIPPED OR CHOPPED PORK

AT CHUCK'S BAR-B-QUE

Chuck's Bar-B-Que is in a building that has been in the same spot since 1986. Chuck Ferrell built his business on quality food and uncompromising integrity. Bible verses are seen on the outside sign, the interior walls, and on the T-shirts of staff members. Chuck's is open Monday through Saturday but closes on Sunday.

Pork shoulder and butts, chipped or chopped, ribs, salads, stew, and stuffed potatoes make up the bulk of the menu, and sandwiches are served with a generous portion of slaw and pickles. There is ample indoor seating, but many get their orders to-go. The combination of consistently good food and friendly service is likely to keep Chuck's going for decades more.

Jody Escoe worked for Chuck for 15 years, learning all the tricks and nuances of the recipes, before buying the restaurant. Escoe was cited as one of the "Top Ten Barbecue Folks" in a book by Annette Thompson called *Alabama Barbecue: Delicious Road Trips*.

905 Short Ave., Opelika, 334-749-4043

22

DINE SUMPTUOUSLY IN VINTAGE SURROUNDINGS AT ZAZU GASTROPUB

Zazu Gastropub opened in late 2015, but the vibe in downtown Opelika is historic. Reclaimed bricks, wide plank flooring, wooden beams salvaged from Opelika's Old Mill, and gas lanterns enhance the ambiance.

Sweet tea fried chicken sandwiches and cornbread are touted as popular menu items, along with poutine, baked oysters, pork spring rolls, and salmon puttanesca. Sunday brunch brings out shrimp and grits, steak and eggs, brioche French toast, and Belgian waffles along with a dozen other mouthwatering choices.

Chef and owner Graham Hage, a former Auburn student, is a very hands-on guy, having done a good bit of the woodwork in the building himself. He incorporates vegetables fresh from the Opelika Grows community garden, makes sausages in-house, and cures bacon on the premises. Chef Hage and his wife, Melissa, love the Broadway musical *The Lion King*. The quirky name of their restaurant comes from one of the musical's main characters.

112 S 8th St., Opelika, 334-203-1747
zazuopelika.com

TIP

Chef Hage also owns Dough Pizzeria in the same block as Zazu Gastropub. Neapolitan and American-style pizzas come out of the wood-fired oven to rave reviews.

104 S 8th St., Opelika, 334-203-1370
facebook.com/doughopelika

23

TASTE SLOW-SMOKED, TEXAS-STYLE BARBECUE

AT BOW & ARROW

Bow & Arrow opened in 2017 and is the second restaurant brainchild of Chef-owner David Bancroft, who was born in Alabama but grew up in San Antonio, Texas. This restaurant reflects Bancroft's South Texas years with its slow-smoked meats, such as brisket, ribs, pulled pork, and turkey, cooked over a live-fire Kudu grill. Uncommon sides like borracho beans, brisket beans, collard greens, and sweet corn rice grace the menu, along with Tex-Mex dishes like tacos, enchiladas, and fajitas. Memaw's Éclair is a signature dessert, and it is as decadent as it sounds.

The rustic interior features mounted deer heads on the walls, metallic (industrial-style) chairs, and concrete floors. Chef Bancroft is a multi-year James Beard Foundation nominee for Best Chef. Bow & Arrow is no ordinary barbecue joint. The food here is exceptional. Bow & Arrow is closed on Monday but opens for lunch and dinner Tuesday through Saturday and for brunch on Sunday.

1977 E Samford Ave., 334-246-2546
bowandarrowbbq.com

EAT BREAKFAST WITH THE LOCALS
AT BYRON'S SMOKEHOUSE

Byron's Smokehouse opened in 1989 and has become a landmark in the area. Originally, it was in a much smaller location, but a former Dairy Queen became available, so the owners moved to the present place on Opelika Road. At Byron's, you place your order and pay at the counter. In a few minutes, a server wanders through the dining room area, calls your name, and delivers your food. The large fluffy biscuits are showstoppers. Families, retirees, students, and many locals frequent Byron's. Breakfast items include house-smoked sausages, eggs, grits, and fried potatoes.

Byron Gulledge and his son Glen opened the restaurant after Byron retired from his first career. They worked side by side for 27 years until Byron's death. Now Glen carries the responsibility. Byron's Smokehouse is open for breakfast Tuesday through Saturday but is closed on Sunday and Monday.

436 Opelika Rd., 334-887-9981
facebook.com/people/byrons-smokehouse/100063649716389

GET YOUR MORNING JAVA AND A SUGAR RUSH

AT MO'BAY BEIGNET CO.

Jaclyn Robinson opened the first Mo'Bay Beignet Co. in downtown Mobile in February 2020. Tripp Skipper is from Mobile. He tasted the beignets and coffee and convinced Robinson that those items would be hits with Auburn University students. The Auburn Mo'Bay opened on North College Street in March 2021 as the first location outside of Mobile.

Beignets are handmade, hand-rolled, hand-fried balls of dough doused with powdered sugar. They were made famous in New Orleans. The Mo'Bay version is different because of the signature dipping syrups that add extra sweetness. Signature syrups are buttercream and cinnamon, but seasonal variations appear throughout the year, such as lemon, strawberry, maple bourbon, and Grandma's chocolate gravy. Chicory coffee, coffee au lait, and a cold brew round out the menu offerings. Everything is made fresh, so you should expect a wait depending on the number of customers in line.

155 N College St., 334-246-3015
facebook.com/mobaybeignetcoauburn

A FEW OTHER POPULAR COFFEE SHOPS IN AUBURN

Big Blue Bagel & Deli
Their Tiger Melt and bagel chips made the list of Alabama Travel's 100 Dishes to Eat in Alabama.
120 N College St.
restaurantguru.com/big-blue-bagel-auburn

The Bean Coffee Shop
They have enormous cinnamon rolls that are made in-house every morning.
140 N Dean Rd.
thebeancoffeeshop.com

One Bike Coffee
It is affiliated with the One Bike Foundation, which raises funds and awareness about multiple sclerosis. Snickerdoodle bread and crack cake are favorites.
2415 Moores Mill Rd., Ste. 130
onebikecoffee.com

The Ross House Coffee
It is in a historic home and has a small menu of breakfast and lunch items. Ross House has expanded to two other locations in Auburn.
150 N Ross St.
rosshousecoffee.com

CHECK OUT ONE OF BO JACKSON'S FAVORITES

AT PANNIE-GEORGE'S KITCHEN

Pannie-George's Kitchen opened in 2005 in Auburn, within sight of the Interstate 85 exit. Owners Lorine Askew and her daughter Mary Counts named Pannie-George after Lorine's parents, Mary (nicknamed Pannie) and George Taylor.

The menu consists of a choice of three meats, seven or eight vegetables, a roll or cornbread, and a drink. You may add a house-made dessert if you are craving something sweet. Diners line up right inside the front door and can see exactly what they are getting as their plates are filled. Call-in and carry-out orders are extremely popular, so you can take your food home or back to the office to enjoy. Sunday may be the busiest day at Pannie-George because several area churches announce the day's menu at the close of their morning services. The mention of sweet potato pie could cause folks to leave before the benediction. Pannie-George's Kitchen has been a favorite of famous Auburn people, such as Bo Jackson, Cam Newton, Coach Pat Dye, and former Auburn coach Tommy Tuberville.

2328 S College St., Ste. 6, 334-821-4142
panniegeorgeskitchen.com

TRY AN ETHNIC DISH
AT HEY DAY MARKET

Hey Day Market is between the Tony and Libba Rane Culinary Science Center and the Hotel at Auburn University. It is a 10,000-square-foot food hall built as a gathering place for students, their friends, and family members or locals who want to sample ethnic foods. Malaysian, Cuban, Italian, Hawaiian, Vietnamese, and Cantonese vendors offer their dishes alongside gelato, smoothies, and all-American classics.

The large green space beside Hey Day Market is perfect for a variety of events, such as benefit nights, holiday celebrations, tailgating on the lawn, and live music performances. Complimentary parking spaces are available on the 2nd and 3rd floors of the South College Street parking deck Monday through Friday after 5 p.m. and all day on Saturday and Sunday. Be aware that Hey Day Market is a cashless venue, so bring your debit and credit cards. Students may use their Tiger Club cards and dining dollars there.

211 S College St., 334-212-9714
heydaymarketauburn.com

TIP

The name for Hey Day Market is derived from an Auburn tradition that dates to the years after World War II when students who had served in the military returned to classes at Auburn.

SATISFY YOUR CURIOSITY ABOUT KOREAN CUISINE
AT CHICKCHICKPORKPORK

ChickChickPorkPork has much more than chicken and pork on its menu, but the name certainly grabs your attention. A unique ordering feature is a button at the table that you push to alert the waiter that you are ready to place your order. This is particularly good since the menu is rather extensive and generally takes time to process. This saves steps for the server and takes the urgency off the diners.

Fried dumplings, served warm and crisp, are a highly recommended appetizer, but others that sound good are a seafood pancake with vegetables called Haemul Pajeon and Korean BBQ pork with vegetables called Bulgogi Salad.

The menu has six categories of entrees, some with puzzling names. The Bento Box is likely the most familiar. With that one, an entrée is served with rice, salad, two fried dumplings, and onion rings. Under the "Popular" category, Beef Bulgogi is reported to be very good. It is sliced, seasoned beef with vegetables.

3810 Pepperell Pkwy., Ste. 2, Opelika, 334-737-5777
chickchickporkpork.com

Chickchickporkpork owners William and Gio Paulk recently opened a fusion dessert café next door called Cheeto's.

Cheeto's
3810 Pepperell Pkwy., Ste. 1, Opelika, 334-363-2877
facebook.com/people/cheetos-fusion-dessert-cafe/100065516828523

REQUEST A SPOT ON THE PATIO
AT LIVEOAKS

The building where LiveOaks is located began as an Amoco gas station in the 1950s. The corner spot is strategically placed to put it in the middle of all that happens in downtown Auburn and almost within sight of Toomer's Corner and its famous oak trees. The indoor space is rustic, casual, and tasteful, but the outdoor patio dining is especially appealing when the weather makes dining there permissible. Convenient parking is available at Berney's Office Supply after 5 p.m. Monday through Friday and any time on Saturday. LiveOaks is open for dinner Monday through Saturday but is closed on Sunday.

The chef has put his personal skills and spin on the menu, which includes Southern favorites alongside blackened tuna, taco burgers, and chicken or pork pad thai. Grilled ears of corn or steak egg rolls make exceptional starters, and the shrimp chimichurri is a specialty salad.

201 N College St., 334-521-5101, liveoaksauburn.com

TIP

The beloved oak trees at Toomer's Corner were poisoned after Auburn won the 2010 Iron Bowl. New trees were planted the same week that the restaurant opened, thus the name LiveOaks.

30

BE TRANSPORTED TO IRELAND

AT IRISH BRED PUB

You don't have to cross the pond to have fish & chips, bangers & mash, or shepherd's pie. Just look for the green two-story building on Railroad Avenue in Opelika with the wraparound balcony. Inside you'll find Old Country vintage charm and décor. Irish Bred Pub is open for lunch and dinner Monday through Saturday and for lunch only on Sunday.

In the tradition of true Irish pubs, the owners strive to create a community atmosphere with food, live music, and games. Trivia nights, poker nights, and plenty of widescreen TVs make this a great spot to come for a night of fun.

The menu includes treats such as Scotch eggs, Guinness burgers, and North Atlantic salmon, but it also offers more familiar Southern favorites: shrimp & grits and muffalettas, to name a few. Reuben egg rolls, pork schnitzel, and Reuben sandwiches add more European tastes, while veggie burgers, chicken sandwiches, and Lee County coleslaw appeal to the less adventurous eaters.

833 S Railroad Ave., Opelika, 334-363-2235
irishbredopelika.com

CELEBRATE YOUR BIRTHDAY WITH A FREE DINNER

AT VENDITORI'S

As a generous gesture, Venditori's offers a free dinner to those who come in on their birthdays, but don't limit yourself to one meal a year. The restaurant serves authentic Italian dishes seven nights a week. Venditori is the Italian word for "sellers," which is the last name of owners John and Kim Sellers.

A wide variety of gluten-free options as well as some vegetarian and vegan dishes will be welcome sights for diners with dietary restrictions. Salad and garlic rolls are served with every entrée, and the Pasta Lover's Special is highly recommended for those who enjoy a variety of pastas and plenty of meat. The dessert menu is full of tempting choices, such as cannoli, spumoni, tiramisu, limoncello mascarpone cake, panna cotta, and more.

Venditori's doesn't take reservations, but you may use their call-ahead feature. Future plans include putting in a bar in the fireplace room to create a cozy space for single diners.

2575 Hilton Garden Dr., 334-826-7360
venditoris-auburn.com

SAVOR FAVORITES FROM BAYOU COUNTRY
AT WALK-ON'S SPORTS BISTREAUX

Louisiana State University (LSU) is often one of Auburn's biggest rivals in sports competitions, but there's no denying the appeal of Cajun and Creole cuisine that has its roots in Louisiana. Now Auburn people can enjoy those classic dishes without making the drive to Bayou Country. Walk-On's Sports Bistreaux, a restaurant with its origins in Baton Rouge, has opened in Tiger Town. Walk-On's was started in 2003 by Brandon Landry and Jack Warner, who were walk-on baseball players at LSU.

Each dish at Walk-On's is made from scratch. Some of the fan favorites are crawfish etouffee, fried alligator, voodoo shrimp & grits, and doughnut bread pudding made from Krispy Kreme Doughnuts. Sports fans who want to eat while watching the games will appreciate the dozens of TVs scattered around the dining area. Stop by soon and try some gumbo, a boudin ball, catfish atchafalaya, or a fresh, hot beignet. Discounts are given to military and law enforcement personnel.

3041 Capps Way, Opelika, 334-822-3430
walk-ons.com

33

TASTE HOMEMADE FLAVOR
AT SHEILA C'S BURGER BARN

Sheila C's Burger Barn serves burgers that taste homemade and are likely to drip with goodness and flavor. That's because the burgers are served with mustard, mayo, ketchup, onion, pickles, lettuce, and tomatoes, unless you order them another way. The menu does offer hot dogs, ham and cheese sandwiches, and chicken sandwiches, but you'd be smart to order what makes the place famous. A milkshake or a root beer float make perfect accompaniments.

Sheila C's is a no-frills place where you are welcome to eat inside or use the drive-through window for call-in orders. You can have your burgers delivered through Tigertowntogo.com. Bear in mind that Sheila's doesn't claim to be a fast-food place, so you might need to wait a few minutes for your freshly-made-when-you-order-it burger. The business has been open for more than twenty years, and loyal followers hope they are settled in for many more.

622 Shug Jordan Pkwy., 334-283-5200

TIP

For more food options, consider Food Truck Fridays in downtown Opelika on the first and third Fridays. Food Truck Fridays have been so popular that Food Truck Saturdays have been added.

TIPS

Locals enjoy farmers markets in the spring, summer, and fall. In Opelika, you will find O Grows across from the Cultural Arts Center on Glenn Street. In Auburn you will find the Market at Ag Heritage Park.

....

Wright's Market is tucked away in an Opelika neighborhood at 603 Pleasant Drive. This 22,000-square-foot grocery store excels in customer service, high-quality meats, and innovation.

603 Pleasant Dr., Opelika, 334-749-1333
wrightsmarkets.com

Gingerbread Village at The Hotel at Auburn University

MUSIC
AND ENTERTAINMENT

BE DAZZLED BY THE TALENT

AT THE JAY AND SUSIE GOGUE PERFORMING ARTS CENTER

The Jay and Susie Gogue Performing Arts Center is a $70 million crown jewel for fine arts in Auburn. Opened in 2019, it has hosted performances by Lee Greenwood, Patti LaBelle, Smoky Robinson, and many others in addition to touring Broadway productions of *Oklahoma, Hairspray, Chicago*, and more.

The Gogue Center consists of the 1,202-seat Woltosz Theatre and the Bill and Carol Ham Amphitheatre with an outdoor space that can accommodate 3,000 to 4,000 concertgoers. The outdoor space is known as the City of Auburn Lawn and Porch. The center also has a stunning, multi-story lobby, box office, rehearsal space, costume and makeup facilities, and elaborate, state-of-the-art audio equipment.

The Gogue Center makes a bold statement about Auburn's dedication to providing excellent fine arts opportunities for university students and for the families who live in Auburn. Season tickets or single performance tickets can be purchased at the box office, by phone, or online.

910 S College St., 334-844-8497
goguecenter.auburn.edu

DISCOVER A RISING STAR

AT THE OPELIKA SONGWRITERS FESTIVAL AND THE SOUND WALL

The Sound Wall is the name of a 1907 Victorian home located on Avenue B in Opelika, which also serves as a rehearsal and performance venue and as an audio/video production studio. The Sound Wall Music Initiative sponsors the Opelika Songwriters Festival held annually in the fall. Listening Room shows, a jazz series, and monthly supper clubs are also a part of the regular lineup of events inside the Sound Wall.

During the yearly festival, as many as nine listening venues are set up around downtown Opelika. Each venue hosts three or four hour-long performances. Rob and Jen Slocumb are the brains behind this event and are passionate about contributing their talents and showcasing the talents of others in this town where they have put down roots. The Slocumbs make their own music under the name of Martha's Trouble. Their Sound Wall Music Initiative aims to support the community through music. The Slocumbs' two teenage children contribute their musical abilities to the cause.

605 Avenue B, Opelika, 334-575-3477
thesoundwallopelika.com
facebook.com/opelikasongwritersfestival

JOIN THE CROWD FOR OKTOBERFEST
AT AG HERITAGE PARK

Oktoberfest at Ag Heritage Park has been called "The South's Favorite Craft Beer Festival." It is a one-day event sponsored and hosted by Ithaka Hospitality Partners. During the hours of the festival, you'll find games, contests, live music, food trucks, and educational presentations about malting, brewing, and distilling. Bring your pet for the wiener dog races and find out how to compete for the titles of Mr. and Miss Oktoberfest. Those who have tried their hand at homebrewing might want to participate in Homebrew Alley to showcase their concoctions and learn from others.

General admission tickets range in price depending on how early they are purchased. Eat, Drink & Be German Package tickets are slightly higher but include a T-shirt and a food voucher redeemable at any of the food trucks. Designated-driver tickets are free.

Parking is available in the hay fields across from the ALFA Pavilion. The 2022 event was held on October 15. Watch social media posts for the 2023 date.

620 N Donahue St., 334-321-3278
auoktoberfest.com

SAMPLE, SHOP, AND LISTEN

AT ON THE TRACKS—A WINE AND CHEESE EVENT

The Opelika Main Street organization has done a remarkable job of drawing positive attention to this historically significant and interesting section of their city. With the addition of murals, planters, parking spaces, and updated storefronts, this has become an attractive mecca for shoppers and those looking for good restaurants. On the Tracks—A Wine and Cheese Event, which happens in the fall, is one of Opelika Main Street's most successful fundraisers. Businesses stay open late, live music performances are scattered throughout the area, and wine and cheese tasting stations are conveniently located for maximum enjoyment. The primary area targets South Railroad Avenue, 8th Street, and 9th Street.

If you miss this date, there are other opportunities to experience a party-like atmosphere along Railroad Avenue. Christmas in a Railroad Town, Touch a Truck, Opelika Main Street on Tap (featuring craft beers), Opelika High School pep rallies, and numerous outdoor concerts appear on the yearly calendar of events.

S. Railroad Ave., Opelika, 334-745-0466
facebook.com/onthetracks

WATCH THE BULL RIDERS OR DANCE TO THE MUSIC

AT AUBURN RODEO

Auburn Rodeo takes place in the spring and fall at Sistrunk Farms. Technically speaking, there IS an actual rodeo, with bareback riding, saddle bronc, and bull riding, and a hysterical wild donkey relay race. Most people, however, come for the headliner musicians who perform throughout the day.

Plenty of food and beverages are available for sale, or you can bring your own coolers and tailgate on the grounds. VIP tickets are worth considering since they include a private viewing area, access to private restrooms, and dinner provided by Jim & Nick's. Those who stay in the tailgate area may bring lawn chairs and umbrellas, but those items are not allowed inside the concert area. A shuttle pass may be purchased, providing transportation from the campus to Sistrunk Farms and back.

Auburn Rodeo has been touted as "the Rowdiest Party in the SEC," so expect a day and night of rambunctious fun and great country music.

Sistrunk Farms, 15400 US 80, Opelika
theauburnrodeo.com

39

GET A CLOSEUP LOOK
AT RAPTORS DURING "FOOTBALL, FANS, AND FEATHERS"

Southeastern Raptor Center, a division of the Auburn School of Veterinary Medicine, hosts a popular event on Friday afternoons at 4 p.m. before home football games called "Football, Fans, and Feathers." This is a cashless event, so plan to pay via check or credit card. Children under three years old are free. Gates open an hour before the show, and seating for up to 350 people is on a first-come, first-served basis. Guests are allowed to bring in their own chairs, food, and drinks.

The program lasts about an hour, and there's very little shade at the Edgar B. Carter Educational Amphitheater, so be sure to bring a hat and wear sunscreen. These presentations allow viewers to see falcons, hawks, and eagles up close. Birds of prey will be free flown from towers and around the amphitheater, and trainers will explain how the various birds survive and what role they play in the ecological system. Each is a permanent resident of the center.

Edgar B. Carter Educational Amphitheater
1350 Pratt-Carden Dr., 334-844-4546
vetmed.auburn.edu/raptor

PITCH A TENT FOR TAILGATING

BEFORE HOME FOOTBALL GAMES

Tailgating under an awning, beside an RV, or from the back of a truck or SUV is a time-honored tradition before home football games on the campus of Auburn University. Many claim their spots beginning early on Friday, or they hire the REVELxp to do all the set-up and take-down chores, although that option is not cheap (https://revelxp.com/auburn). The best spots for tailgating are the ones nearest Jordan-Hare Stadium and include the hayfields on Donahue Drive, the intramural fields on Biggio Drive, the pines at Weagle Woods, Graves Amphitheater, and Ag Heritage Park.

Fans arrive long before kick-off dressed in orange and blue and begin exchanging "War Eagle" greetings with fellow fans while digging into a pregame feast. Some tailgaters prepare dishes at home and transport them in coolers, while others pick up tailgate packages of barbecue, chicken fingers, and all the trimmings from places such as Moe's Original BBQ, Full Moon BBQ, Jim & Nick's, or Lucy's.

Auburn University Athletics Department, 855-282-2010
aotourism.com/football/5/tailgating

Auburn IMG Sports Network hosts the official radio broadcasts of the Auburn Tigers games. Andy Burcham is the voice of the Auburn Tigers, and Jason Campbell will become an analyst in the fall of 2023.

auburntigers.com/sports/auburn-sports-network

BUY A TICKET FOR A PERFORMANCE

AT THE OPELIKA CENTER FOR THE PERFORMING ARTS

The Opelika Center for the Performing Arts might be in a high school auditorium, but Opelika High School's auditorium is a truly exceptional facility. In the 30 years since it opened, this performing arts center has hosted 20 international orchestras, 50 Broadway touring productions, 9 operas, 21 ballets, and 21 jazz concerts.

The auditorium has 1,150 seats with each providing an unobstructed view of the stage. Southern Union State Community College is adjacent to Opelika High School, so both schools have the advantage of this wonderful venue. The Arts Association of East Alabama (EastAlabamaArts.org) is the umbrella organization that plans and brings the topnotch performers to Opelika in partnership with the Opelika Board of Education.

Residents of Auburn, Opelika, and surrounding towns are fortunate to have high-quality entertainment options available and the opportunity for their children to be inspired to practice and excel.

1700 Lafayette Pkwy., Opelika, 334-749-8105
eastalabamaarts.org/opelika-center-for-the-performing-arts

TRY OUT FOR A PART
AT AUBURN AREA COMMUNITY THEATRE

Children, youth, and adults who love to be on stage or merely want to hone their acting skills have a wonderful resource in Auburn. Acting classes are offered for children ages 5 to 18, and sessions teaching dramatic acting for adults also appear on the calendar of events. The goal of Auburn Area Community Theatre is two-fold. It seeks to educate and create opportunities for participation. One- and two-week summer camps are extremely popular and often foster a lasting interest in theater arts.

Participants in the community theater provided entertainment last year at Holiday Walk in the Woods at Kreher Preserve, which is destined to become an annual event. Two full-length shows featuring children and youth are presented every year. The Jan Dempsey Community Arts Center, where performances have taken place for many years, is undergoing extensive renovations, so be sure to watch closely for the location of this year's performances.

222 E Drake Ave., 334-246-1084
auburnact.org

43

LISTEN TO COUNTRY MUSIC

AT OLD 280 BOOGIE AT STANDARD DELUXE IN WAVERLY

The Standard Deluxe is a design and silkscreen print shop in Waverly, which is about a 15-minute drive down Highway 280 from Auburn. On a selected Saturday in the spring and fall, the population of Waverly swells to a thousand or more for a few hours of music and fun. People from miles around bring lawn chairs and blankets. They choose from the various food vendors, who start serving at noon, and peruse the crafts offered for sale by area artisans before the show starts at 2 p.m. The show lasts until about 8:30 p.m. and requires a ticket.

Performances take place on an outdoor stage and happen whether it is sunny or rainy. If you buy tickets before the specified deadline, they are several dollars cheaper. Boogie weekends conclude with a Boogie Brunch on Sunday morning. The musical genre is country with splashes of country-soul and country-blues thrown in for good measure.

1015 Mayberry St., Waverly, 334-826-6423
facebook.com/waverlyboogie
standarddeluxe.com

PEEK INSIDE BEAUTIFUL BUILDINGS
DURING THE LOVELIEST VILLAGE CHRISTMAS TOUR

The Auburn Preservation League hosts a holiday fundraiser that provides glimpses inside homes and buildings that you normally only get to admire from a distance. The buildings and homes on the tour reflect the values of historic preservation while also being examples of designer expertise.

For one admission price of $15.00 (the 2022 price), visitors are allowed to visit all the sites on the tour, and tickets may be purchased at any of the sites. Sometimes the owners are present, but often members of the Preservation League serve as volunteer guides and answer questions. Homes are beautifully decorated for the season, and sites such as churches or historic homes have people on-site to explain the significance and particular features.

The Loveliest Village Christmas Tour in Auburn coincides with the Gingerbread Village display at the Hotel at Auburn University and Opelika's Victorian Front Porch Christmas Tour. That allows visitors to enjoy a full day of holiday festivities.

Auburn Preservation League
facebook.com/loveliestvillagechristmastour

45

FIND ORIGINAL CRAFTS
AT SYRUP SOPPIN' DAY IN PIONEER PARK AT LOACHAPOKA

If the weather cooperates, the Syrup Soppin' Day at Pioneer Park in Loachapoka draws thousands. Admission is free, but it costs $5 to park in one of the remote lots. Complimentary shuttles carry visitors back and forth. Loachapoka is a 10-minute drive from downtown Auburn.

The main connection to syrup happens near the front of the festivities, with a horse going in a circle to cause a squeezing apparatus to extract syrup from bundles of sugar cane. The resulting syrup is bottled and sold the same day. Those bottles always sell out quickly.

Live musicians perform throughout the grounds. In addition to modern arts and crafts, you will find corn-shelling, ice cream making, demonstrations of pioneer games, and plenty of food vendors. Hours for this fall event are 7 a.m. to 4 p.m.

Lee County Historical Society, 6500 Stage Rd., Loachapoka, 334-887-3007
leecountyhistoricalsociety.org/syrup-soppin

TIP

The Lee County Historical Society Museum in Pioneer Park is spread out over nine buildings and adjoining gardens. The museum is open Wednesday through Saturday all year long.

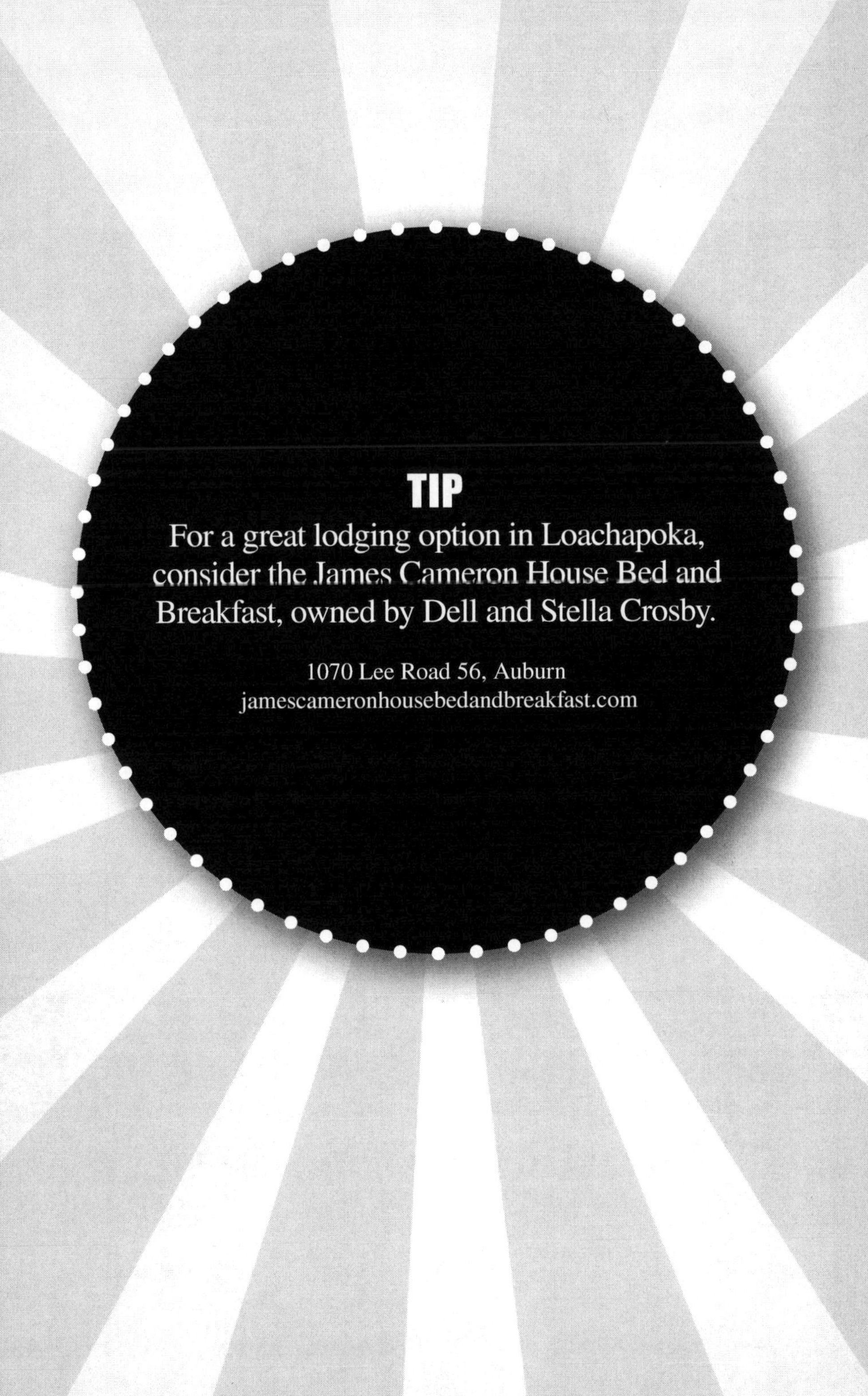
TIP
For a great lodging option in Loachapoka, consider the James Cameron House Bed and Breakfast, owned by Dell and Stella Crosby.
1070 Lee Road 56, Auburn
jamescameronhousebedandbreakfast.com

46

ADMIRE THE GINGERBREAD VILLAGE INSIDE THE HOTEL
AT AUBURN UNIVERSITY

The elaborate Gingerbread Village that has become a much-anticipated holiday sight in Auburn is a joint effort between the students at the new Tony & Libba Rane Culinary Science Center and the culinary staff of the Hotel at Auburn University. It is said to be the largest gingerbread village in the region, and I suspect that includes most of the state of Alabama.

During the construction of the village, an astonishing quantity of ingredients is used. It is astounding what can be accomplished with 280 pounds of gingerbread, 130 pounds of icing, 90 pounds of candy, and 1,000 hours of manpower and creativity. The most recent version featured replicas of Samford Hall, Jordan-Hare Stadium, Auburn Chapel, Agricultural Heritage Park Pavilion, Toomer's Corner, the Culinary Science Center, Langdon Hall, Storybook Farm, and more.

The village is unveiled after the yearly Christmas parade and is set up throughout the remainder of the month of December. There is no admission charge for viewing the village.

241 S College St., 334-821-8200
auhcc.com

TIP

Auburn and Opelika have at least a half-dozen locally owned bakeries displaying exceptional cakes, cookies, and sweet treats. Each one has its own specialties and loyal customers.

Gourmet Tigers
231 N Dean Rd., 334-821-9222
gourmettiger.com

Sweet As Cakes
409 Green St., 801-521-0328
facebook.com/taniacobine

Honey Badger Bakery
2205 Columbia Dr., 334-444-5749
facebook.com/honeybadgerbakeryauburn

J.A.M. (Just Add Milk) Cakery
2135 Interstate Dr., Ste. 182, Opelika, 334-498-5722
jamcakery.com

Tart & Tartan
117 S 8th St., Ste. 203, Opelika, 334-748-9075
facebook.com/tartandtartan

STEP BACK IN TIME
AT A VICTORIAN FRONT PORCH CHRISTMAS TOUR

The second weekend in December allows you to step back in time to 1899. For five days, houses in the Northside Historic District turn their porch lights on and decorate with mannequins in period costumes, greenery, lights, and holiday cheer for the Victorian Front Porch Christmas Tour.

The festivities begin at the Heritage House Inn on the corner of 2nd Avenue and North 8th Street and continue down North 8th and 9th Streets. Caroling quartets, handbell groups, and choirs of elementary schoolchildren lend their voices and enthusiasm to the scene. Both *Better Homes & Gardens* and *Southern Living* magazines have declared this to be one of the best holiday events in the Southeast.

On Friday, Sunday, Monday, and Tuesday during the designated weekend, the tour is a self-driving one and lasts from 5 p.m. to 9 p.m. On Saturday evening, 8th and 9th Streets are blocked off, and it becomes a walking tour. At least 60 homes now participate in the tour, which began in 1993.

N 8th and 9th Streets, Opelika, 334-704-3068
facebook.com/opelikavfpt

The Heritage House Inn is an elegant place to stay in Opelika during the Victorian Front Porch Christmas Tour weekend or anytime. Make reservations well in advance because there are only five guestrooms.

714 2nd Ave., Opelika, 334-552-3052
heritagehouse1913.com

CATCH BEADS
AT THE MARDI GRAS PARADE IN DOWNTOWN AUBURN

The downtown streets close at 2 p.m., and the parade begins at 3 p.m., with the timing being a sure indication that this is a family-friendly event. The Krewe de Tigris Mardi Gras Parade starts at the intersection of Thach Avenue and South College Street, proceeds down Thach to Gay Street, on to Tichenor and College, then back to Thach. Your only responsibility is to dress in your best gold, green, and purple finery and be ready to catch moon pies of every flavor, throws, and tons of beads. Enjoy floats, motorcycles, unicycles, the Grand Marshall, Auburn stars (such as the reigning Miss Auburn), musicians, and much more.

Many houses in area neighborhoods join the fun by decorating their front lawns in celebration of "Yardi Gras." The Auburn Downtown Merchants Association often hosts an accompanying Krewe Krawl, in which those who wish may buy a wristband that will entitle them to discounts on food and merchandise at participating stores and restaurants.

downtownauburnonline.com

TIP

Follow the Auburn Downtown Merchants Association for other planned events, such as Sip & Shop, the Downtown Cruise-In Car Show, and First Fridays.

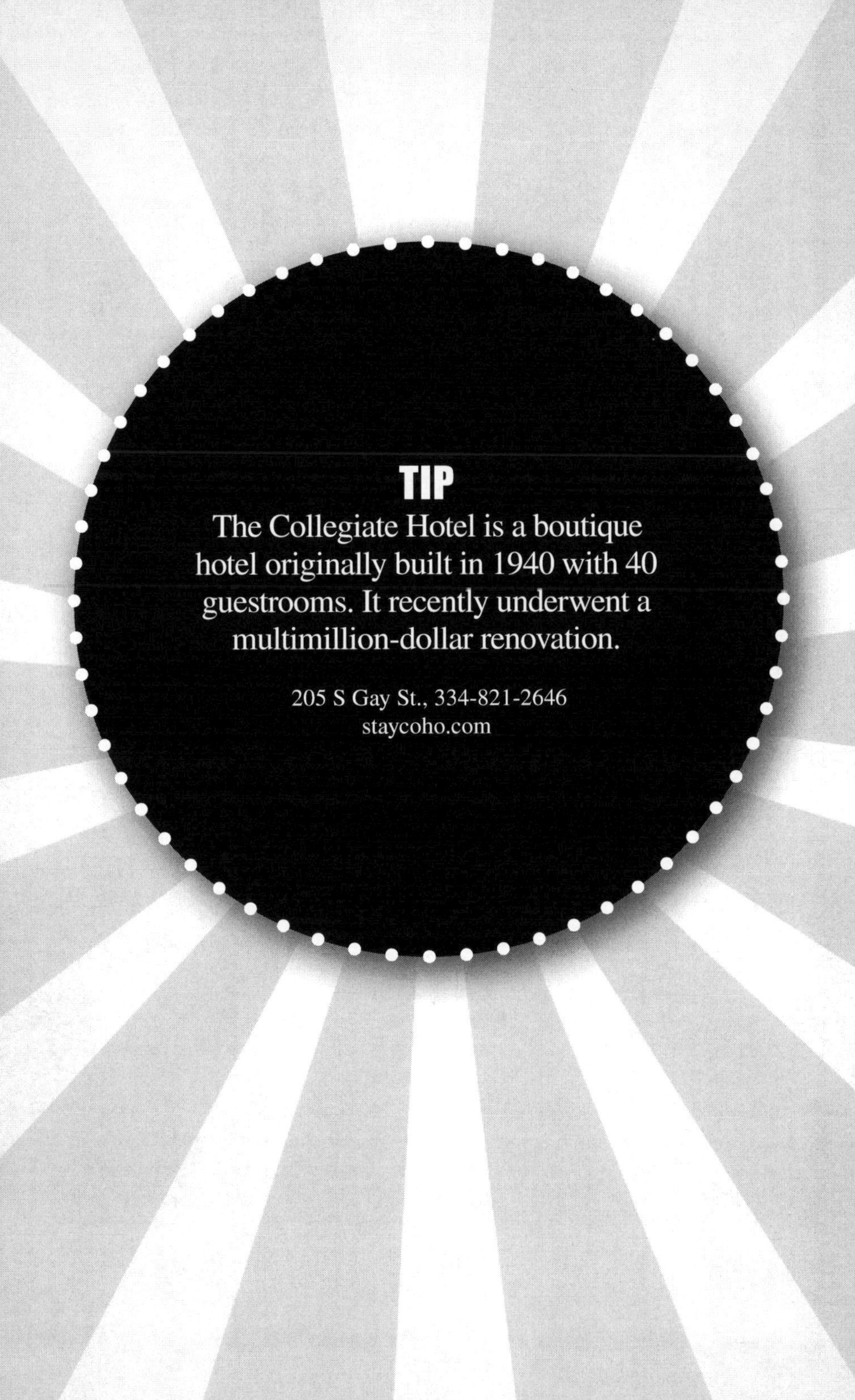
TIP
The Collegiate Hotel is a boutique hotel originally built in 1940 with 40 guestrooms. It recently underwent a multimillion-dollar renovation.
205 S Gay St., 334-821-2646
staycoho.com

FIND A SPOT

AT MONKEY PARK FOR THE SUMMER SWING CONCERT SERIES

The Summer Swing Concert Series in Monkey Park is a popular family event that takes place on Tuesday evenings from early May to early August. Take your lawn chairs and food from home if you like, but food is also available for purchase at the concerts. The Opelika High School Band Boosters prepare hamburgers and hot dogs for a reasonable price as a fundraiser. The concert series is a great time to see your neighbors, and everyone loves an Elvis impersonator. A playground is near the concert pavilion to attract the children. This is a family-focused event. The park has lots of trees, and the concert is held along the banks of the Rocky Brook Creek, which runs through the park.

A miniature train called the Rocky Brook Rocket is also a favorite with children. It has been a fixture in the park since 1955. Other park events include the Flashlight Egg Hunt during Easter season, a fall festival, and a children's carnival.

Municipal Park, Park Rd., Opelika, 334-705-5549
opelika-al.gov/614/municipal-park

TIP

Municipal Park is known locally as Monkey Park. During the 1950s, the park was home to eight spider monkeys. Wooden monkey statues were added to the park in 2016 in honor of the monkey days and the fun they brought.

HEAD TO KIESEL PARK
IN THE SPRING FOR AUBURN CITYFEST

CityFest in Auburn is one of the town's most anticipated events. It is Auburn's largest free outdoor festival, and there's fun and great food for all ages. CityFest happens rain or shine on the last Saturday in April and generally runs from 9 a.m. to 4 p.m. The event is sponsored by the Auburn Parks and Recreation Department.

Live music, a juried art show, crafts vendors, children's activities, balloons, clowns, and everything you would expect for a rollicking good time happens at CityFest. Aubie, Auburn's beloved mascot, often makes an appearance, along with birds of prey from the Southeastern Raptor Center. The children's art tent is very popular.

Kiesel Park has a 2.5-mile walking trail, a garden, a pond on the grounds, as well as the Nunn-Winston House. The house was built by Samuel Nunn in the 1850s and is a lovely example of antebellum Greek Revival architecture. The house is available as an event venue.

520 Chadwick Lane, 334-734-2650
https://auburnalabama.org/parks/facilities/kiesel-park

Cheerleaders and Aubie
Credit Getty Images

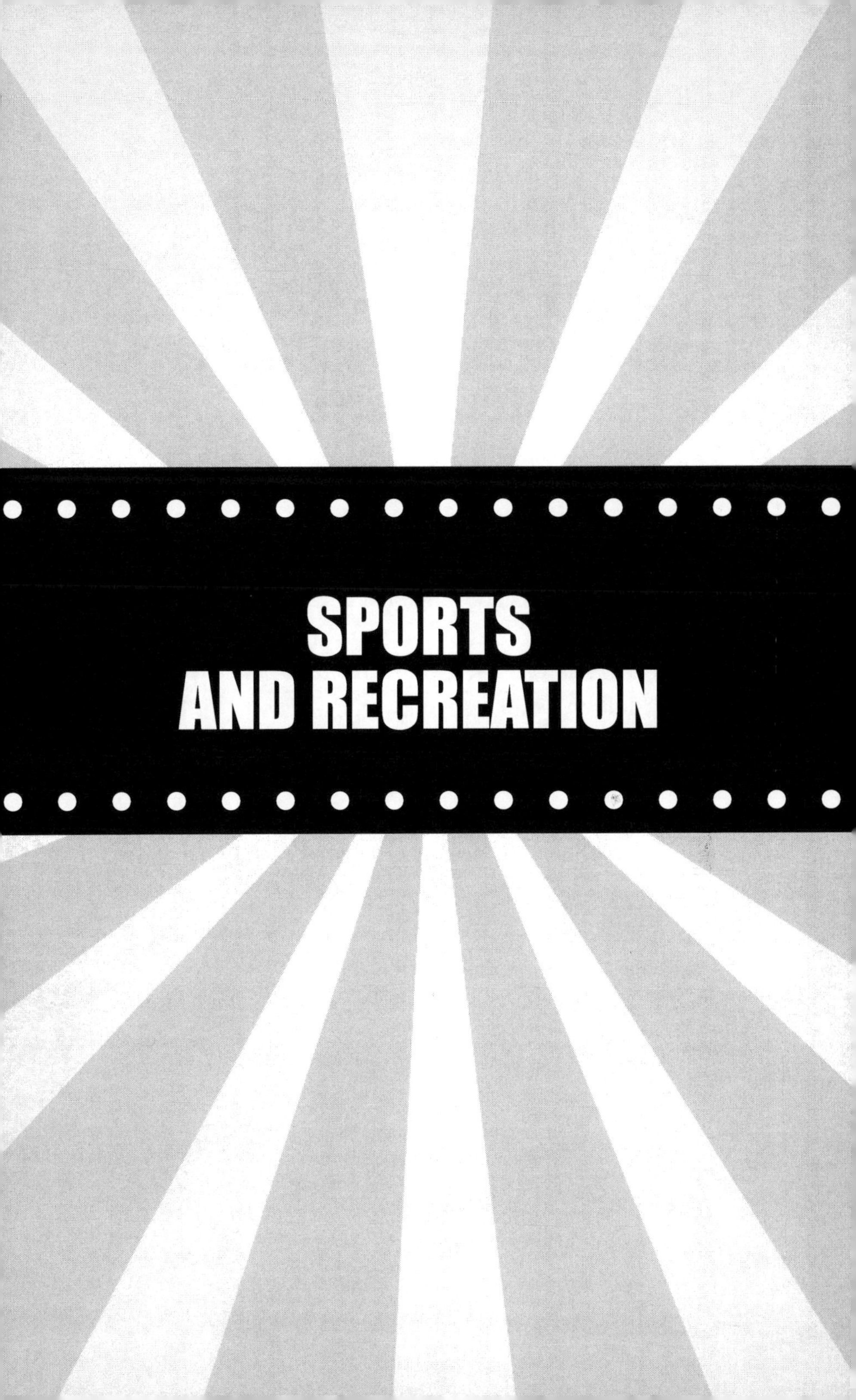

SPORTS AND RECREATION

51

SURROUND YOURSELF WITH NATURE

AT KREHER PRESERVE AND NATURE CENTER

Kreher Preserve and Nature Center, also known as the Louise Kreher Forest Ecology Preserve, is a place to soak up the wilderness environment, to exercise with a vigorous hike, or to attend an educational program. Kreher Preserve is designed as a place for discovery.

Six miles of trails take you past a pond, a butterfly garden, a waterfall, a wildflower trail, a serenity fountain, and a turtle pond. A human-size eagle's nest and beaver lodge are lots of fun for children. Recent sessions in the outdoor classroom included a seminar about black bears and another about campfire cooking. A covered pavilion with seating for 80 and a 150-seat amphitheater are available for event rentals.

The preserve hosts events such as A Holiday Walk in the Woods, Nature Babies, Family Discovery Hikes, Nature Walks, AUsome Amphibians and Reptiles (in the fall), and In the Garden with Cyndi. It is completely free to walk the trails, but special programs involve a small fee.

2222 N College St., 334-844-8091
wp.auburn.edu/preserve

SOLVE THE MYSTERIES
AT AUBURN ESCAPE ZONES

Auburn Escape Zones has been described as "the most interactive, thought-provoking hour of fun you can legally have in East Alabama!" Five rooms are available, each with its own theme. Teams of as many as eight people are locked in, with 60 minutes to solve a set of problems, find clues, and crack the code. A Game Master introduces the scenario and monitors the group's progress via cameras set up on the inside. Recent rooms have included Blackbeard's Brig, with pirate problems; Imprisoned, with a prison theme of an innocent person facing the electric chair; the Cabin, where someone has been bitten by a rattlesnake and team members must get to the anti-venom; Vault, where members are locked inside a bank vault; and Supervillains and Puzzler. New themes rotate in every five to six months.

The cost is $25 per person per experience. Auburn Escape Zones is closed Monday through Wednesday but is open Thursday through Sunday. Reservations are recommended.

1234 Commerce Dr., 334-329-7088
auburnescapezones.com

53

GO MOUNTAIN BIKING OR CAMPING
AT CHEWACLA STATE PARK

Chewacla State Park encompasses 696 wooded acres, which include Chewacla Falls cascading from a height of 30 feet, the 26-acre Chewacla Lake, eight hiking trails, and much more. Besides being a popular spot for picnics and family recreation, Chewacla is well known among mountain bikers. In partnership with the state park system, Central Alabama Mountain Peddlers (CAMP) has worked to make Chewacla an excellent place for mountain biking. The park is home to the state's only wall ride. The Great Wall of Chewacla has a 15-foot arc and a 70-degree angle.

In the lake, you will see kayaks and canoes, as well as swimmers and those who choose to fish from the bank. Geocaching attracts enthusiasts, and hikers enjoy both easy and challenging trails.

Six rustic stone cabins, each with a wood-burning fireplace, are available for rent, and nine primitive camping sites can be found in the park. For those who prefer more comfortable accommodations, Chewacla has 36 modern campsites with full water, electric, and sewage hookups.

124 Shell Toomer Pkwy., 334-887-5621
alapark.com/parks/chewacla-state-park

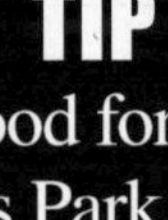

TIP

Auburn parks good for families and dog walking are Dinius Park, Town Creek Park, Hickory Dickory Park, Felton Little Park, Kiesel Park, Martin Luther King Park, Moores Mill Park, and Sam Harris Park.

auburnalabama.org/parks

HIT THE TARGET
AT TUMBLE TREE DISC GOLF

The Tumble Tree Disc Golf course at the Opelika Sportsplex & Aquatic Center is a suitable place to practice your aim and get plenty of exercise without spending much money. The course itself is free to use. Participants just need to bring plenty of discs and water to stay hydrated while playing the 18 holes.

Tumble Tree is dog-friendly, so feel free to bring your dog on a leash and be sure to clean up after your pet. You and your dog (and your teammates) will walk small hills, make your way through trails, and cross over bodies of water. There is a practice tee and a large open field for warming up before starting a round.

You are welcome to sign up for tournaments, which are hosted at Tumble Tree throughout the year. The course gets consistently good ratings from those who play on other courses around the state. A course map is provided by the Opelika Parks and Recreation Department.

1001 Andrews Rd., Opelika, 334-705-5560
aotourism.com/recreation/35/tumble-tree-disc-golf-course

55

LEARN TO PLAY A POPULAR NEW SPORT

AT THE OPELIKA PICKLEBALL FACILITY

Pickleball is said to be the fastest-growing sport in America, and Auburn and Opelika players have joined the throngs of enthusiasts. Loosely defined as a cross between tennis and badminton, pickleball involves two or four players hitting a lightweight ball over a three-foot-high net using solid-faced paddles.

Twenty-four regulation-sized, covered courts are available for use twenty-four hours a day, seven days a week. The last players of the day are asked to turn the lights off when they leave. Parking is plentiful, there's no charge for playing, and restrooms and concessions are nearby.

The Opelika Pickleball Club hosts tournaments in the spring and fall called "Paddles at the Plex," and members are eager to teach beginners the fundamentals of the sport. Details can be found at opelikapickleball.com.

1001 Andrews Rd., Opelika, 334-705-5560
opelika-al.gov/852/opelika-pickleball-facility

BRING YOUR BINOCULARS

TO ONE OF THE PIEDMONT PLATEAU BIRDING TRAILS

Lee County has four spots of the 40 listed on the Piedmont Plateau Birding Trails, with many more within an hour's drive. Piedmont Plateau is part of the Alabama Birding Trails. The spots in Lee County are Chewacla State Park, Louise Kreher Forest Ecology Preserve & Nature Center, Lee County Public Fishing Lake, and Opelika Wood Duck Heritage Preserve & Siddique Nature Park.

At the Kreher Ecology Preserve, 122 different species have been observed by birders in recent years, and at the Wood Duck Heritage Preserve, the number is 203. Chewacla is a great place to find woodland songbirds, Mississippi kites, swallows, vultures, hawks, ospreys, eagles, waders such as egrets, ibis, and herons, and a wide variety of warblers. Lee County Lake is where you are likely to find bluebirds, nuthatches, woodpeckers, and ducks, such as Canvasback, Ruddy, Redhead, and Bufflehead. The website provides specific information about the best viewing spots in each of those areas.

alabamabirdingtrails.com/trails/piedmont-plateau

ESCAPE THE RAIN AND COLD WITH INDOOR FUN

AT GOOD TIMES BOWLING

If the weather is cold and wet but you would really like to have some fun with your friends, you are in luck. At Good Times Bowling on East Glenn Avenue in Auburn, you can play arcade games, eat a full meal, try to figure your way out of two escape rooms, or roll a few strikes.

Prices are by the hour. If you just want to bowl and it is Monday through Thursday, that will be the least expensive rate. Most will want to have access to everything inside Good Times Bowling. The highest per-hour prices are charged on Friday and Saturday.

The menu goes far beyond popcorn, candy, and soft drinks. This impressive menu offers pizza, wings, wraps, sandwiches, loaded potato skins, corn nuggets, and much more. The desserts are tempting, too, with such items as cheesecake, funnel cake "fries," and cinnamon sugar donut holes.

Good Times opens at 4 p.m. Monday through Friday and at noon on Saturday and Sunday.

Glenndean Shopping Center, 750 E Glenn Ave., 334-539-3131
goodtimesbowling.com

IMPROVE YOUR AIM

AT THE OPELIKA COMMUNITY ARCHERY PARK

Bowhunters and archery enthusiasts are giving rave reviews about the new Community Archery Park at Opelika's Spring Villa. The park is free and open to the public from 7 a.m. to sunset year-round.

Twelve covered bays with targets placed at distances of 20 to 60 feet are available for improving your skills, and bowhunters will appreciate the raised platform, which creates conditions like those when hunting from a tree stand.

The surrounding Spring Villa Park is special, too. Within its 350 acres, you will find restrooms, an outdoor volleyball court, walking trails, picnic tables, grills, 30 campsites with full hook-ups, a camping lodge that can be rented for group gatherings, and an antebellum house known as the Penn Yonge House.

The Penn Yonge House was built by former slave and master bridge builder Horace King. The grounds of the park once served as a working Southern plantation, and it was placed on the National Register of Historic Places in 1978.

1474 Lee Rd. 148, Opelika, 334-705-2308
opelika-al.gov/623/spring-villa-park

GRAB SOME FRIENDS
AND HEAD TO TIGERTOWN SPORTS

One of the newest just-for-fun attractions in Opelika is Tigertown Sports on Parker Way near Lowe's. An 18-hole putt-putt golf course might be the marquee draw, but other opportunities for friendly competition are available here as well. If you enjoy lawn games, you will find several, as well as a virtual golf simulator. Even though Auburn is several hours away from the beach, Tigertown Sports has created three sand beach volleyball courts, which provide a great group exercise venue.

Tigertown Sports has a full bar with pizza and beverages for sale, so you will not have to leave to find food and refreshments. It is designed to be family friendly and is conveniently located just off Interstate 85 at exit 58. Visitors will want to sign up in advance for time slots with the various activities. Whether you are putting, spiking, or merely sipping and watching from the patio, this is a destination like no other in the area.

615 Parker Way, Opelika
tigertownsports.com

SINK A PUTT
AT GRAND NATIONAL GOLF COURSE IN OPELIKA

Grand National Golf Course consists of three 18-hole courses: Links Course, Lake Course, and Short Course. Two of those courses are considered by *USA Today*'s Golfweek to be among the ten best courses in the entire state of Alabama. Mike May, an international travel and golf writer, puts Grand National in the top four of Alabama's Best. Readers of *Golf World* claim that it is the #1 public golf facility in America. High words of praise continue to pour in for this beautiful property on the 600-acre Lake Saugahatchee in Opelika. Thirty-two of the 54 holes are situated around the lake. Grand National plays host to NCAA Division 1 Men's and Women's Championships and the LPGA and PGA tours.

Tee times can be reserved on the website. Prices are $50 for the short course and $87 for the Lake and Links courses. Amenities include putting greens, a practice range, a Pro Shop, lockers, and nearby dining and lodging.

3000 Robert Trent Jones Trl., Opelika, 334-749-9042, rtjgolf.com/grandnational

TIP

The Four-Diamond Auburn/Opelika Marriott Resort and Spa adjacent to the golf course is a lovely accommodation option.

3700 Robert Trent Jones Trl., Opelika, 334-741-9292
marriott.com/en-us//hotels/csgab-auburn-marriott
-opelika-resort-and-spa-at-grand-national/overview

DRIVE THE AUBURN FLORAL TRAIL IN THE SPRING

A major project of the Auburn Beautification Council in the spring is their annual Auburn Floral Trail. The 14-mile-long self-guided trail is divided into two sections. The North Trail is 3.5 miles long, and the South Trail is 10.5 miles. Both pass through Auburn neighborhoods and in front of homes, providing recognition for homeowners who have spent countless hours making their yards beautiful. Drivers and cyclists will see signs posted along the route.

The official trail dates encompass five to six weeks when spring blooms are at their peak. Trail visitors can expect to see azaleas and camellias of many varieties and colors and flowering trees, such as dogwood, pear, cherry, and plum.

Trail maps are available at City Hall or can be downloaded from the Floral Trail website.

P.O. Box 3366, 334-501-7367
auburnbeautification.com/floral-trail
auburnalabama.org/environmental-services/auburn-floral-trail

TIP

Crenshaw Guest House offers a variety of accommodation configurations and is about a block from the railroad tracks on North College Street, within a short walk of Toomer's Corner.

371 N College St., 334-821-1131 crenshawguesthouse.com

CAST YOUR ROD AND CATCH YOUR SUPPER

AT LEE COUNTY PUBLIC FISHING LAKE

Lee County Public Fishing Lake has 130 acres of well-managed water filled with bass, bluegill, sunfish, catfish, and crappie. The Lake Store sells live and artificial bait and tackle, plus it has restrooms and snacks to make your fishing hours more productive. You can bring your own boat and launch it at the boat ramp or rent one there with a trolling motor big enough to get you around the lake at a comfortable pace. You will need an Alabama fishing license, which you can purchase at the store.

This lake is also a good place to enjoy peace and tranquility and do some birdwatching, since it is on the Alabama Birding Trail. The lake is only six miles from Opelika, so it is very convenient for a quick time on the water and the possibility of bringing home a string of fish for supper.

321 Lee Rd., Opelika, 334-745-6563
outdooralabama.com/alabama-public-fishing-lakes-pfls/lee-county-pfl

TIP

Truly serious anglers will want to drive less than an hour from Auburn and fish at Lake Martin, which encompasses 40,000 acres and has 800 miles of shoreline.

lakemartin.com, explorelakemartin.com

IMPROVE YOUR BACKHAND
AT YARBROUGH TENNIS CENTER

The Yarbrough Tennis Center is a joint project between the City of Auburn and the Auburn University Athletics Department. It is a state-of-the-art facility that was dedicated in 2007 and was named the Professional Tennis Registry Public Facility of the Year a few short years later. The Auburn University men's and women's tennis teams compete at Yarbrough Tennis Center, but it is also open to the public, and courts can be rented at very reasonable rates.

Thirty-four courts can be found at the center: 16 are clay courts, 12 are outdoor hard courts, and six are indoor hard courts. Memberships are available, but non-members are welcome to call ahead and see if a court is open.

Sign up for clinics or private lessons or head out to Yarbrough Tennis Center to watch an SEC matchup and cheer on the Tigers.

1717 Richland Rd., 334-501-2920
auburnalabama.org/parks/facilities/yarbrough-tennis-center

WATCH THE EAGLE SOAR
AT JORDAN-HARE STADIUM

About 25 minutes before kickoff at each home game, a majestic golden eagle is released from the top of the stadium. It circles the stadium in jaw-dropping fashion before landing at midfield, drawn by a handler with an enticing bait. (The bait is a carefully crafted piece of leather, but it works for training the eagle.) The crowd draws out the word "Warrrrrrrrrrrrr" until the eagle lands, at which time every Auburn fan yells "Eagle!" This is one of the most spectacular pre-game events in college football.

Jordan-Hare Stadium boasts the largest video board in college football, with its 10,830-square-foot Jumbotron, and its current seating capacity is 87,451. The stadium is named in honor of Cliff Hare, a member of the first Tigers team who became a chemistry professor on campus, and Ralph "Shug" Jordan, beloved head football coach from 1951 to 1975.

251 S Donahue Dr., 334-844-4750
auburntigers.com/facilities/jordan-hare-stadium/11

TIP

The first Iron Bowl played at Jordan-Hare Stadium was on December 2, 1989. "Iron Bowl" is the term used for the annual contest between the football teams of Auburn University and archrival University of Alabama.

65

ADD YOUR RUMBLE TO THE JUNGLE

AT NEVILLE ARENA

The atmosphere inside Neville Arena when the men's basketball team plays a game ranks among the best in the entire country. The support and enthusiasm of the fans give the team a tremendous advantage. Students make a lot of noise when the other team has the ball, and thcy try thcir best to make distracting moves during free throws. On the other hand, when an Auburn player stands at the free-throw line, everything goes silent waiting for that ball to drop through the net. Head coach Bruce Pearl gets the credit for creating the whole "Jungle" scenario, and it has worked to everyone's advantage.

There are a lot of seats available for students, but the number is still limited. That has led to tent cities appearing before big games, where students camp out overnight to be one of the lucky ones to get one of the first-come, first-served seats. Go experience the rumbling jungle for yourself.

11 Heisman Dr., Auburn
auburntigers.com/facilities/neville-arena-basketball/1

TIP

Auburn Arena has 9,121 seats and opened for the 2010–2011 season. It was renamed Neville Arena in honor of Bill and Connie Neville after they gave the single largest gift in the history of Auburn Athletics.

JOIN THE THRONG FOR TIGER WALK

BEFORE HOME FOOTBALL GAMES

Precisely two hours before the kickoff of a Saturday home football game at Jordan-Hare Stadium, team members, the coaching staff, cheerleaders, and Aubie will walk from the Athletics Complex, down Donahue Drive, and into the stadium. Throngs of fans, who begin gathering an hour beforehand to stake out the best vantage points, will cheer wildly, hoist young kids onto their shoulders, take tons of cellphone photos, try to shake hands or get a high-five from players, and do their best to exhibit their love and support for the home team. It is a time-honored tradition that began in the 1960s.

All the players and coaches are dressed fashionably for the occasion. Some have headphones in their ears and wear serious game faces, while others engage with the crowd in exuberant ways. The band plays the fight song, and the cheerleaders wave their pompoms. It only lasts a few minutes, but everyone gets fired up for the game.

From the Athletics Complex, down Donahue Drive to Jordan-Hare Stadium
auburntigers.com/ sports/2019/3/28/tiger-walk.aspx

TIP

If your pet has an accident or gets sick while in town, Auburn School of Veterinary Medicine's Bailey Small Animal Teaching Hospital has you covered with excellent facilities and expertise.

Small Animal Teaching Hospital Emergency Services
1220 Wire Rd., 334-844-4690
vetmed.auburn.edu/animal-owners/emergency-services

CATCH A HOMERUN BALL
AT PLAINSMAN PARK (SAMFORD STADIUM–HITCHCOCK FIELD)

Baseball fans can hardly wait to hear the words "Play ball!" during the spring of every year. The Auburn Tigers Baseball team made it to the College World Series in Omaha, Nebraska, in 2022, so expectations are high for future teams to provide thrilling games full of clutch plays.

The designers of Plainsman Park borrowed elements from Wrigley Field, Camden Yard, and Fenway Park to create a facility that is consistently listed among the best for college baseball. Fans enjoy a gigantic video board and a state-of-the-art sound system. They can look at the Wall of Fame in the outfield remembering the feats of former Auburn greats Bo Jackson, Gregg Olson, Frank Thomas, and Tim Hudson, and it would be hard to miss the 30-foot-high wall in left field, referred to as the Green Monster. The seating capacity at Samford Stadium–Hitchcock Field, the specific name for the venue, is 4,096.

351 S Donahue Dr., 334-844-9750
auburntigers.com/facilities/plainsman-park/9

TIP

Auburn fan gear and concessions are available for purchase at Plainsman Park, but transactions are cashless, meaning credit/debit cards or Tiger Cards are the only accepted forms of payment.

TEST YOUR INNER DAREDEVIL SKILLS

AT THE NEW AUBURN–OPELIKA SKATE PARK

Helmets are a must, and padded, covered clothing is highly recommended when you ride your bike, strap on a pair of rollerblades, or balance your body on a skateboard while defying gravity at Auburn and Opelika's impressive Skate Park, the only park of its kind in the area. Bowls, halfpipes, and yards of pavement await enthusiasts who wish to hone their skills no matter whether you are a beginner or an advanced skateboarder.

The park, located at the Indian Pines Golf Course, is the perfect place for outdoor exercise, and best of all, it's completely free. The facility is open from sunrise to sunset seven days a week. Take note, however, that on Saturday mornings from sunrise to noon the park is taken over by remote-controlled cars. Stop staring at your phone, grab some friends, and head to the Skate Park for hours of fun.

900 Indian Pines Dr., Auburn
auburnalabama.org/parks/facilities/skate-park

69

ROLL TOOMER'S CORNER
AFTER A BIG AUBURN VICTORY

The tradition of throwing toilet paper in the trees and power lines came when Auburn was playing archrival Alabama in November 1972. Alabama was unbeaten and ranked #2 in the nation. Terry Henley, a beloved member of that 1972 team, told reporters, "We're going to beat the Number 2 out of Alabama." A miracle happened, and Auburn ran two blocked punts back for touchdowns, leading to a 17–16 win over the Tide. That victory did indeed knock Alabama down from their #2 ranking.

The game was played at Legion Field in Birmingham, but the victory was celebrated by students and townspeople who took rolls of toilet paper to Toomer's Corner and exuberantly hurled them into the trees. Even now, all an Auburn person has to say is "Punt, Bama, Punt," and everyone knows what the words mean. That is where the fans still go after Auburn victories, and a large supply of toilet paper stays ready for such occasions.

The intersection of College Street and Magnolia Avenue
in the center of downtown Auburn.

70

SUPPORT A GREAT CAUSE
BY RIDING IN BO BIKES BAMA

Bo Bikes Bama has evolved into an annual charity bike ride that raises money for the Governor's Emergency Relief Fund. The event began in 2013, when Bo Jackson came to Cordova, Alabama, for a one-day ride to raise money for one of the hardest hit areas during the April 27, 2011, tornado outbreak in which 62 tornadoes were tracked within an 18-hour period, 240 people were killed, and several entire communities were leveled.

Bo Jackson had the unique ability to garner support for this effort, especially among Auburn people, because he was the university's second Heisman Trophy winner in football, and he was a star baseball player. He went on to play both professional baseball and professional football. Nike created an advertising campaign in 1989 and 1990 called "Bo Knows." Later, Bo titled his autobiography *Bo Knows Bo.*

Riders in Bo Bikes Bama may choose either a 62-mile route or a 22-mile ride. This is not a race, so riders will not be timed.

bobikesbama.com

ZIPLINE

ACROSS THE ALABAMA/GEORGIA STATE LINE

Less than an hour's drive from downtown Auburn, you can be on the banks of the Chattahoochee River in Columbus, Georgia. At the Blue Heron Adventure Park, it is possible to strap on the proper harnesses and zip through the air for 1,200 feet across the river and across the state line from Georgia to Alabama. Once on the Alabama side, you will soar another 500 feet along the shoreline before going back across the Chattahoochee for 1,100 feet to the starting point. This is the only dual zipline in the entire United States that connects two states.

If you look down while you are over the water, you will likely see whitewater rafting, kayaking, and tubing being enjoyed below. Whitewater Express offers adventures for beginners through advanced thrill seekers.

1000 Bay Ave., Columbus, GA, 706-321-4720
chattahoochee.whitewaterexpress.com

TIPS

Plan another couple of hours to be informed and inspired at the National Infantry Museum in Columbus.

1775 Legacy Way, Ste. 235, Columbus, GA, 706-685-5800
nationalinfantrymuseum.org

....

For lodging in a luxurious boutique hotel that was once a grist mill on the banks of the Chattahoochee River, make reservations at City Mills Hotel.

1801 1st Ave., Columbus, GA, 706-940-0100
citymillscolumbus.com

Mural at Museum of East Alabama

CULTURE AND HISTORY

LEARN SURPRISING HISTORY AT THE MUSEUM OF EAST ALABAMA

The Museum of East Alabama, which opened in 1989, is a relatively small, regional museum where you can spend 30 minutes or several hours immersing yourself in the history of Opelika and the five counties surrounding it. Glenn Buxton is the museum's director and is a passionate storyteller who can make the 5,000 collected artifacts have meaning and significance. Admission is free, but donations are gladly accepted.

Some intriguing exhibits are about the area's connection to the Creek Indians, the textile mills, and the World War II POW camp that was in Opelika. Murals adorn both sides of the museum's exterior. The latest one was painted by Chris Johnson and completed in 2022. That mural incorporates a Creek Indian chief who lived around Eufaula, a buggy from the 1920s, an Auburn University flag, a 1905 steam traction engine, Pepperell Mills, Booker T. Washington (who founded Tuskegee Institute), a train signifying the importance of the railroad, plus baseball players from the Opelika Owls minor league team.

121 S 9th St., Opelika, 334-749-2751, eastalabama.org

FUN FACT

The movie *Norma Rae*, for which Sally Field won an Academy Award for Best Actress in 1980, was filmed in Opelika.

73

WATCH FOR GHOSTS
AT SALEM-SHOTWELL COVERED BRIDGE

The Salem-Shotwell Covered Bridge is adjacent to Opelika Municipal Park. It was built originally in 1872 near the community of Salem and crossed the Wacoochee Creek. A tree fell on the bridge in 2005 and much of the structure collapsed into the creek. Area residents jumped into action to salvage as much of the structure as possible. The Opelika Kiwanis Club undertook the project of relocating and rebuilding the bridge. In 2007, it officially reopened. The reconstructed bridge is shorter than the original.

Salem-Shotwell Bridge has quite a few paranormal tales associated with it. One story involves a young woman who invited a young man to meet her at the bridge in the 1960s. When he didn't show up, she hung herself there. Another story claims that a mother and two young children died when the original bridge collapsed. It is said that if you leave candy or toys at the edge of the bridge at night, those ghost children will come out and collect them.

700 Park Rd., Opelika, 334-705-5560
https://en.wikipedia.org/wiki/salem-shotwell_covered_bridge

RECALL GREAT AUBURN ATHLETES
AS YOU WALK THE TIGER TRAIL

When you're walking down one of the two streets that converge to form Toomer's Corner, College Street and Magnolia Avenue, you will notice diamond-shaped, granite plaques embedded in the concrete sidewalks. Those plaques are engraved to honor Auburn greats: athletes, coaches, and administrators, in every imaginable sport. Football, basketball, swimming, track, equestrian events, softball, gymnastics, baseball, soccer, and volleyball are just a few of them. This is a combined effort of the Auburn Chamber of Commerce and the Auburn University Athletics Department. Take a stroll and find your favorites.

The trail was launched in 1995. It now numbers more than 100 honorees, and a new class is added every year. The entire Auburn community is invited to attend the Induction Ceremony, which generally takes place in the fall. Tickets are available through the Chamber of Commerce.

College Street and W Magnolia Avenue, 334-887-7011
aotourism.com/arts-and-culture/5/tiger-trail-of-auburn

TIPS

Eight Auburn greats have been honored on the campus with statues: Pat Dye, Shug Jordan, Cliff Hare, Pat Sullivan, Bo Jackson, Cam Newton, Charles Barkley, and Frank Thomas.

....

Famous Auburn graduates who were not sports stars include Kay Ivey, Fob James, Tim Cook, Octavia Spencer, Taylor Hicks, Jimmy Wales, Ken Mattingly, and Jan Davis.

75

MARVEL AT INTRICATE SPECIMENS

INSIDE THE MUSEUM OF NATURAL HISTORY

The Auburn University Museum of Natural History is primarily a research museum. The staff includes curators of birds, fishes, insects, mammals, amphibians, reptiles, fossils, and the collection currently has about two million specimens.

The museum is in the Biodiversity Learning Center beside M. White Smith Hall, slightly north of West Samford Avenue. Public tours are offered on the first Wednesday of each month at 5:30 p.m. and last about an hour and a half. The tour is free, but it is important to register in advance.

In the spring, coinciding with March Madness in the college basketball world, the museum has a fun event called March Mammal Madness, which simulates matchups between various animals. Beginning in mid-February, participants can pick up their brackets, fill them out, and turn them in. By following through the website, you see how the winning animals are advancing.

Biodiversity Learning Center, 381 Mell St., 334-844-4132
aumnh.auburn.edu

WATCH AUBURN THEATRE STUDENTS PERFORM
AT THE TELFAIR B. PEET THEATRE

Auburn's Department of Theatre offers degree programs leading to a Bachelor of Arts in Theatre and a Bachelor of Fine Arts in Music Theatre, Performance, Management, or Design Technology. Those students need a place to use what they're learning. Both the Mainstage, which has 349 seats, and the Black Box Theatre, which has seating for around 120, are performance spaces and classrooms for Auburn students pursuing those degrees. As a result, the public is invited to enjoy six productions a year in those theatres, from August through May.

The Black Box Theatre is so named because it looks like a black box with black walls, black floors, and a black curtain system around the room. It also has a tension grid system around the ceiling that is capable of holding 90,000 pounds of lighting, cables, speakers, and other performance-enhancing equipment. The seating configuration of the room can change according to the needs of the performance, so this is an experimental space for students.

350 W Samford Ave., 334-844-4154
cla.auburn.edu/theatre

TOUR
THE JULE COLLINS SMITH MUSEUM OF FINE ART

The Jule Collins Smith Museum of Fine Art is accredited by the American Alliance of Museums, a distinction held by less than 6 percent of museums in the nation.

The museum has six changing galleries, but the permanent collection houses Audubon prints, works by many artists from or with ties to Alabama and the South, works representing American Modernism, pottery, ceramics, and works by European and American artists from the 18th to the 21st centuries. There is an auditorium and a gift shop. The seven acres encompassing the museum include walking trails, an English-inspired formal area, and outdoor sculpture.

The entry to the museum has a stunning focal point. The Dale Chihuly chandelier is made up of more than 600 individual pieces of hand-blown glass that took four days to install. The museum is closed to the public on Monday but has regular hours Tuesday through Sunday. Admission is free, but donations are gladly accepted.

901 S College St., 334-844-1484
jcsm.auburn.edu

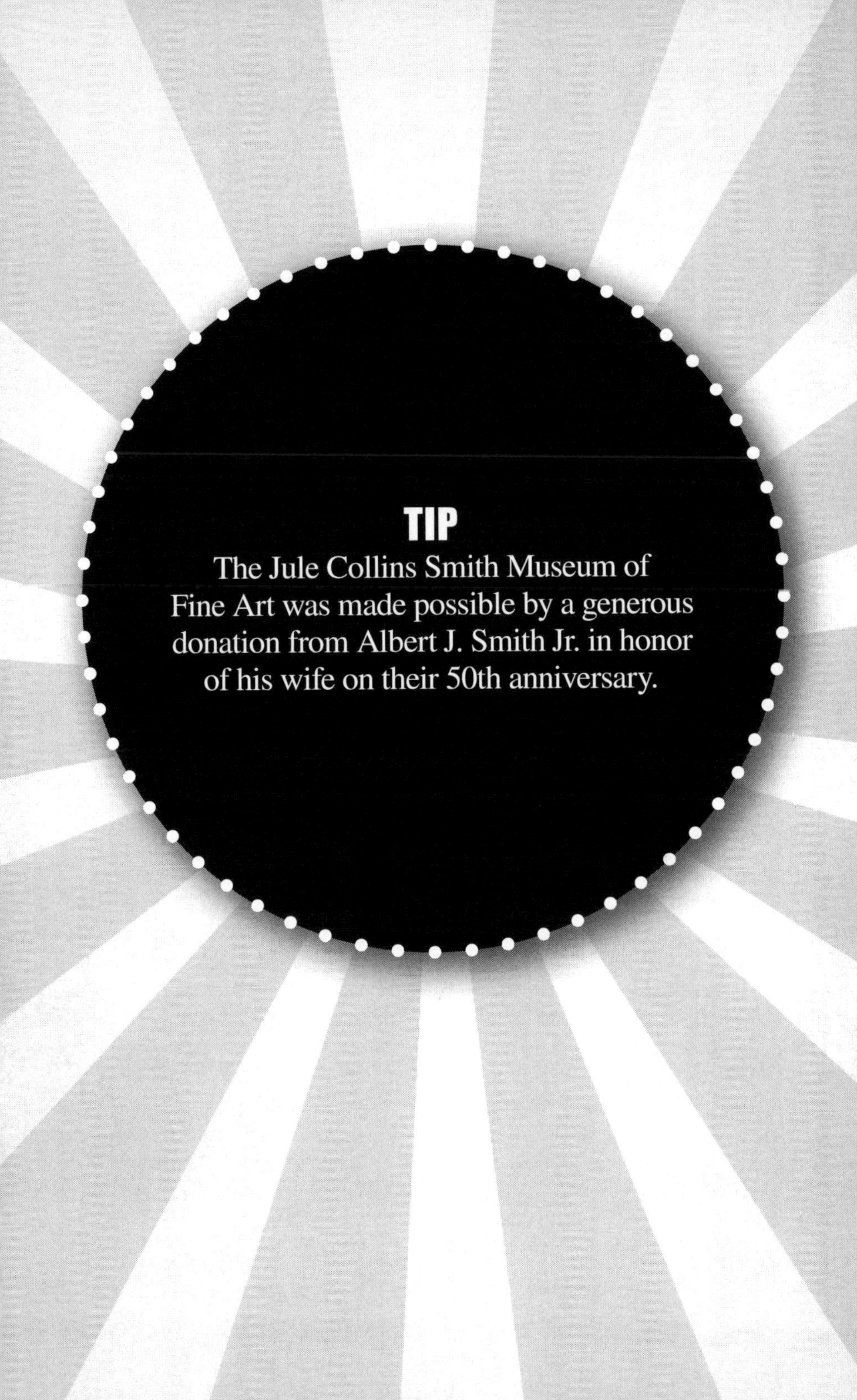
TIP
The Jule Collins Smith Museum of
Fine Art was made possible by a generous
donation from Albert J. Smith Jr. in honor
of his wife on their 50th anniversary.

FIND THE 11 PUBLIC MURALS IN AUBURN AND OPELIKA

Unexpected pops of color appear in whimsical places throughout Auburn and Opelika. Each brings beauty to otherwise mundane walls and reveals a sense of pride in the businesses they adorn.

In Auburn, look for dancing bears behind Moe's, a slice of pizza at Little Italy, tigers and eagles near Momma Goldberg's, ocean waves across from Wrapsody on North College Street, and the orange and blue War Eagle painted beside J & M Bookstore.

In Opelika, find the large "Bless You" sign, the butterfly wings, and the yellow umbrella in the middle of downtown, the Greetings from Opelika mural in front of the library, and the large storytelling murals on both sides of the Museum of East Alabama.

Public art fosters a sense of community, allows a town to develop its unique personality, and enhances the lives of locals and visitors. The number of murals continues to grow in Auburn and Opelika. Stay on the lookout for these works of art when you're out and about.

aotourism.com/blog/22181/visit-the-murals-of-auburn-opelika

BE SURPRISED
AT THE MUSEUM OF WONDER IN SEALE

Less than an hour from Auburn but a little bit challenging to find, you will discover one of those places you have to see to believe. Former Auburn student Butch Anthony, now a renowned artist of extraordinary works, has his home (a one-room cabin he built by hand), the Museum of Wonder, and a studio and gallery there. You'll turn down a gravel driveway and pass a lake, forest, fields, and occasional metal sculptures. Most think it's worth the effort to see the world's largest gallstone or a Sasquatch footprint.

Anthony coined the term "Intertwanglelism" to describe his art and one-of-a-kind creations. He is best known for his intertwangled portraits, which are old photographs or paintings by other artists that he has painted skeletons on top of along with sayings or quotes that he hears and collects in his journals. You will also see three-dimensional pieces made up of found or donated objects, such as bones, tractor parts, or photos, and spot-painted skeletons and taxidermized animals. Tours are by appointment only.

970 Alabama 169, Seale
museumofwonder.com

TIP

The Drive-Thru Museum, located about a mile down the road and also managed by Butch Anthony, is open and free of charge 24 hours a day, 7 days a week.

DIG DEEPER INTO AFRICAN AMERICAN HISTORY

AT NEARBY TUSKEGEE UNIVERSITY

Less than a 30-minute drive from Auburn you will come to Tuskegee University, formerly known as Tuskegee Institute. The campus itself is lovely and impressive, but five specific sites provide important insights into the contributions of African Americans hailing from this part of Alabama.

The Oaks served as the home for Booker T. Washington when he was the first principal of the school that was eventually called Tuskegee Institute. The George Washington Carver Museum is undergoing a multimillion-dollar renovation, but it is scheduled to reopen in the spring of 2024. The Legacy Museum gives a lot of history of Tuskegee Institute and information about medical issues that were prevalent when the institute was founded. The Tuskegee Institute National Historic Site outlines the accomplishments made by the Tuskegee Institute.

The Tuskegee Airmen National Historic Site can be toured in Hangar One at Moton Field Municipal Airport. The Tuskegee Airmen had to fight the enemies of the United States in World War II but also the enemy of racism.

1212 W Montgomery Rd., Tuskegee, 334-727-3200
nps.gov/tuai/index.htm

TIP

In Tuskegee you will also find the Commodore Museum, where Tuskegee native and Institute alum Lionel Ritchie and his group The Commodores recorded several of their well-known hit songs.

208 E Martin Luther Hwy., Tuskegee, 334-724-0777

TAKE A CLASS AND SEE WORKS BY LOCAL ARTISTS

AT ART HAUS

Art Haus, located at the corner of South Railroad Avenue and North 5th Street in Opelika, is designed to house working studio spaces for local artists, to have gallery space for displaying completed works, and to provide a teaching area where artists can share their skills with interested students. It is not open for regular tours, but the Facebook page lists upcoming classes, art markets, and exhibits so you can stay alert for opportunities to take a class and show your support for the Opelika art scene.

The building housing the Art Haus was a former church building. J. and Ginger Stern liked the location and could see the potential for the church building as well as a nearby fellowship hall and two adjacent houses. They engaged the expertise of Bahzad Nathjaven, past chairman of the Auburn University architecture program, who made the present facility a reality by adding natural light and utilizing wood and bricks with local historical significance.

500 N Railroad Ave., Opelika
opelikaarthaus.com

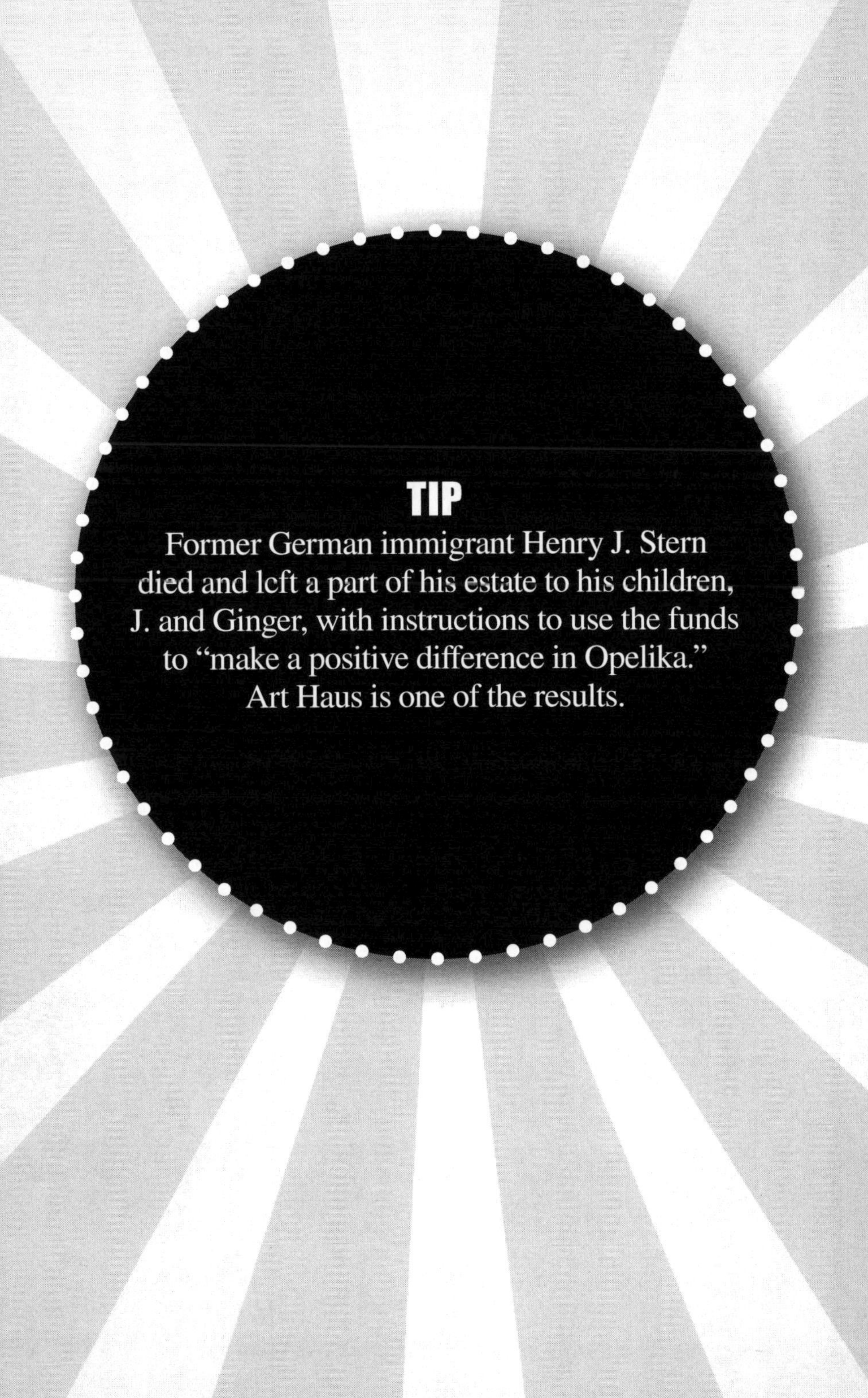
TIP
Former German immigrant Henry J. Stern died and left a part of his estate to his children, J. and Ginger, with instructions to use the funds to "make a positive difference in Opelika." Art Haus is one of the results.

82

VISIT PEBBLE HILL

AND LEARN OF ITS TIES TO THE CIVIL WAR AND AUBURN

Pebble Hill, an antebellum cottage built in 1847, serves as the home of the Caroline Marshall Draughon Center for the Arts and Humanities on Auburn's campus. Self-guided and guided tours of the home are by appointment only and can be arranged by emailing cmdcah@auburn.edu. The Third Friday Poetry Series is a free event and takes place from 6 p.m. to 8 p.m. at the house.

Pebble Hill has several very interesting ties to people and events in Auburn. It was originally built by Nathaniel J. Scott for his family. Scott's half-brother, John J. Harper, founded the town of Auburn. Scott and some other Methodist men in Auburn started East Alabama Male College in 1856, which eventually became Auburn University.

In April 1865, Union soldiers known as Wilson's Raiders looted Pebble Hill, but thanks to astute planning on the part of the owners, most of the valuables the looters were hoping to find had been buried on the property. Fortunately, the soldiers left without burning the house down.

101 Debardeleben St., 334-844-4946
cla.auburn.edu/cah/pebble-hill

TIPS

The Caroline Marshall Draughon Center for the Arts and Humanities is named after a much beloved former first lady of Auburn University. She was known as a gracious hostess for countless university events.

....

If you live near Auburn and would like to take a course without tests or grades, consider enrolling in one of the affordably priced courses for adults over the age of 50 through the Osher Lifelong Learning Institute.

Boykin Community Center, 400 Boykin Auburn, 334-844-3146
auburn.edu/olli

Aubie cookie at Cakeitecture

SHOPPING AND FASHION

FIND VINTAGE AND NEW VINYL RECORDS
AT 10,000 HZ RECORDS

Russell and Hannah Baggett moved to Auburn from the triangle area of North Carolina (Raleigh, Durham, Chapel Hill) where there were numerous record shops. Russell's record-buying hobby led to the realization that Auburn and Opelika needed to fill a void in this area. He began by setting up pop-up record shops in local coffee shops. That success led to the brick-and-mortar store, which became a reality in a former warehouse building on 1st Avenue in downtown Opelika.

10,000 Hz Records stocks a large collection of new and used vinyl records but goes further to offer merchandise such as turntables, speakers, polyvinyl sleeves, hi-fi gear, and pertinent accessories. Baggett will often buy records that customers bring in.

The shop has a space for live performances, record signings, and gatherings with like-minded music lovers. It is open every day, but it's a good idea to call before you go just in case the urge strikes Baggett to take a day off.

717 1st Ave., Ste. A, Opelika, 334-748-9074
10000hzrecords.com

SPEND HOURS SEARCHING FOR TREASURES

AT ANGEL'S ANTIQUE & FLEA MALL

Angel's Antique & Flea Mall has space for more than 450 vendors and encompasses over 68,000 square feet. In the words of one of the staff members, "If you're looking for something in particular, it's very likely to be here. But good luck finding it." The hunt is 99% of the allure.

Since opening in 2002, it has grown in popularity and is rated among the best antique malls in the South by magazines and newspapers. Toys, dishes, radios, baskets, furniture, tea sets, books, lamps, mirrors, vintage signs, and collectibles of every kind line the rows, so plan to allow plenty of time for browsing. Unlike an outdoor flea market, Angel's Antique and Flea Mall has the advantage of indoor air conditioning with wheelchair access and straight aisles. Angel's offers free coffee and a sitting area for those who need to pace themselves. Located at exit 62 off Interstate 85, it is open every day of the year, except Easter, Thanksgiving, Christmas, and New Year's Day.

900 Columbus Pkwy., Opelika, 334-745-5574 or 334-745-3221
facebook.com/aaafm

BUY EVERYTHING ORANGE AND BLUE

AT THE AUBURN UNIVERSITY BOOKSTORE

The ground floor of Haley Center is the epicenter for souvenir shoppers on Game Day Saturdays on the Plains. The Auburn University Bookstore is on the way to Jordan-Hare Stadium, and it carries every conceivable item of fan gear you could imagine.

Décor items adorned with artwork by Julia Gash, Under Armour clothing with the Auburn logo, books, gifts, decals, flags, jewelry, hats, and much more can be found at Haley Center. Samford + Donahue is a line of clothing and merchandise also available there. Samford and Donahue are two well-known streets that intersect on the Auburn campus. That corner is said to be where academics and athletics meet. Individual schools on the campus are also represented with clothing, so you can find shirts adorned with logos of the schools of Nursing, Engineering, Agriculture, Pharmacy, among others.

Normally, the Auburn University Bookstore is only open Monday through Friday, but Game Days are a huge exception. The store is transitioning to a cashless operation, so plan to use your credit cards.

1360 Haley Center, 334-844-4241
aubookstore.com

Buc-ee's is the wildly popular new phenomenon that has recently opened a location in Auburn. It is famous for dozens of gas pumps, brisket, fudge, gifts, clothing, and squeaky-clean restrooms.

buc-ees.com

CHOOSE THE PERFECT TOUCH FOR YOUR HOME
AT ARTIFACTORY

Artifactory is a one-stop shop for anyone wanting to decorate their home in a tasteful, elegant, and unique style. From the basics of furniture, lighting, rugs, and antiques to the finishing touches of artwork, dishes, and linens, Artifactory has an array of choices.

Michael and Rebecca Thompson, both graduates of Auburn University, are the owners. Their loyalty to their alma mater is evident in various parts of the store, such as with the ceramic tigers and eagles, the tiger-themed pottery, and orange and blue or tiger throw pillows. Michael has some amazing eagle paintings for sale in the store. I doubt you'll find anything with a houndstooth pattern here. Unexpected items might include the luxurious loungewear, doormats, tooth fairy pillows, or baby gifts. Artifactory hosts open house events throughout the year and a popular occasion called "Sips & Stems," where participants create a beautiful table arrangement to take home.

2298 E University Dr., Ste. A-102, 334-209-1107
artifactoryauburn.com

TIP

To find the perfect fashion touch for your wardrobe, check out Magnolia James Boutique.
1957 E Samford Ave., Ste. B, 334-521-0063, magnoliajamesboutique.com

SHOW YOUR LOYALTY TO AUBURN

WITH ITEMS FROM AUBURN ART

If it's orange, blue, or a combination of the two; if it represents an iconic place or event in Auburn history; if it is an Auburn-themed bracelet or pair of earrings; or if it is a piece of tableware you need for game-watching parties; you'll find it at Auburn Art in the heart of downtown Auburn. Beautifully framed photos line the burnt orange walls, and one of the most treasured pieces is an autographed #7 jersey worn by Pat Sullivan, Auburn's first Heisman trophy winner.

If you want to show your Auburn pride in your office, rec room, or kitchen, Auburn Art is where you need to go for the perfect painting or dish. Some items that are ONLY sold at Auburn Art include a Toomer's Lemonade candle, a War Eagle wedding plate, a frame specifically sized for Auburn University diplomas, or a Victory at Auburn University Toomer's Corner plate. A blanket made from Auburn T-shirts is another popular gift. Framed vintage photos are great to give Auburn graduates from the early years.

102 N College St., 334-887-7788
auburnart.com

CARRY ON A LONG-STANDING TRADITION

BY VISITING J & M BOOKSTORE

J & M Bookstore was first opened by George Johnston and Paul Malone in 1953. Johnston bought out Malone in the 1960s, but the name of the store remained the same. The store building dates to 1878, when it was known as Burton's. Auburn may have undergone changes since 1953, but J & M Bookstore has remained in its same location offering great service and merchandise to generations of Auburn students.

J & M Bookstore currently has an additional location on South College Street. George Johnston's two sons now own the business, with Trey running the downtown location and Skip managing the one two miles farther down South College Street. Originally, J & M Bookstore was one of the main places where students went to buy their books for classes. Nowadays, class texts are in digital form. Recently the family made the decision to stop selling books and focus on apparel and souvenirs, such as stickers, decals, drinkware, artwork, bags, jewelry, cards, and hundreds of shirts.

115 S College St., 334-887-7007
jmbooks.com

TIPS

The War Eagle Wall a few steps from J & M was painted by George Johnston back in the 1980s but is actually owned by Ronnie Ware of Ware Jewelers.

....

Auburn University's past names are East Alabama Male College, Agricultural & Mechanical College of Alabama, and Alabama Polytechnic Institute. It is said to have the happiest students in the country.

89

MAKE YOUR SPECIAL SOMEONE SMILE WITH A GIFT FROM WARE JEWELERS

A dream of many Auburn coeds through the years has been to receive an engagement ring from Ware Jewelers when her boyfriend proposes. Lamar and Libby Ware opened the store in 1946, and it is the oldest continuously operated family jewelry store in the area. It is now into its fourth generation of Ware family members. Its reach has expanded beyond Auburn to Opelika, Montgomery, and Spanish Fort, Alabama.

In the beginning, the Wares sold small household appliances, in addition to jewelry, and were the first to sell color televisions in Auburn. Eventually, jewelry took over as the focus of the business, and now they carry such widely recognized industry brands as David Yurman, Roberto Coin, John Hardy, Lagos, and Judith Ripka. Ware Jewelers is the kind of place where today's grooms come in to buy rings at the same place where their grandfathers bought rings for their grandmothers.

111 S College St., 334-821-7375
warejewelers.com

GATHER, READ, AND SAMPLE TREATS
AT WELL RED COFFEE, BOOKS & WINE

Well Red Coffee, Books & Wine sells books, coffee, wine, and dessert. The books are both new and used, and many have regional connections. The coffee might vary from roaster to roaster, but a current favorite comes from Non-Fiction Coffee Company. An impressive wine list is available at Well Red, and wine tastings are a regular fixture on the calendar.

Richard and Crystal Tomasello, both Auburn graduates, opened their store in June 2020. The atmosphere is comfortable and homey with nooks for studying or catching up on some reading. Free Wi-Fi is available, and the outdoor space strung with lights is perfect for gathering with friends and devouring one of the delectable treats created by the in-house pastry chef. Both vegan and gluten-free sweets are on the menu, along with cookies, cheesecake, quiche, cinnamon rolls, and charcuterie plates. Author book signings and visits are much anticipated events scheduled at Well Red, so be sure to follow their Facebook page to learn more.

223 Opelika Rd., 334-246-3021
wellredau.com

ADD STYLE TO YOUR WARDROBE
AT BEHIND THE GLASS

Behind the Glass, a beautiful store near Hamilton's on Magnolia, has a very eclectic collection of shoes, accessories, books, candles, and apparel. Most of all, it is a cutting-edge location for women's fashions. Owner Donna Young and her daughter Chloe have chosen merchandise that lives up to words such as "boho," "flirty," "sophisticated," and "quirky," which have been used to describe it.

The two-story building makes the showroom and display areas open and expansive. Brands such as Steve Madden, Free People, and DAYDREAMER lend a barrage of patterns and colors to the space.

Behind the Glass has swimwear, pajamas, hair clips, headbands, handbags, dog toys, eye masks, bath products, party dresses, and journals. If you are shopping for a stylish outfit for yourself or a gift for your best friend, you are likely to find appealing options at Behind the Glass. The store has been serving Auburn for more than 32 years with no plans for slowing down.

168 E Magnolia Ave., 334-826-1133
btgauburn.com

ENTERTAIN AND DECORATE GLAMOROUSLY

WITH HELP FROM THE GALLERY ON RAILROAD

The Gallery on Railroad resides in the historic Strother Purves building, a 19th-century saloon and brothel. Owner Debbie Purves was the first to renovate a building on Railroad Avenue. The Gallery opened in May 1980. In the summer of 2022, the restaurant next door burned down, causing a lot of smoke damage to the Gallery. The Gallery moved a few doors down temporarily but will reopen in its gleaming, freshly redecorated original space.

The Gallery is well known as a source for custom framing, fine art, and decorative art, but it extends to gifts, women's clothing, specialty gourmet foods, and home accessories. With their tagline in mind—"Live passionately, decorate luxuriously, and entertain beautifully"—the Gallery on Railroad has a line of exclusive brands that they feature in the store. Frog Hollow Farm, Savannah Bee Company, Teresa Alacrim Linens, and Bella Cucina Gourmet are just a few. Follow the Facebook page for the latest information.

809 S Railroad Ave., Opelika, 334-749-2462
thegalleryonrailroad.com

ENJOY BROWSING IN AN ELEGANT SETTING

AT WAKEFIELD HOME

Wakefield Home is a truly elegant store to visit and browse. You will find it in the vintage building that once housed Alabama Office Supply. In fact, the office supply company still does business in the back. They don't stock the merchandise, but customers may order and come in the next day to pick up their purchases. Members of the Asbury family have owned the building since 1946. Wakefield Home is owned by Wake and Joan Asbury, and their home furnishings boutique has been in business for more than ten years.

As you walk through Wakefield Home, you will hear soothing music and smell some very appealing scents. The furniture on display has both antique and new pieces. There are paintings, accessories, light fixtures, lamps, and bedding. This is also a great place to find a special gift. In keeping with the upscale emphasis of the store, you will find a beautiful selection of women's clothing, accessories, and jeweled headbands.

201 S 8th St., Opelika, 334-203-1513
wakefieldhomeal.com

WALK OUT WITH A BEAUTIFULLY WRAPPED PACKAGE

AT SOUTHERN CROSSING

In July 2022, Southern Crossing was forced to move from its original location on Railroad Avenue when an adjacent restaurant burned to the ground and caused damage to the beautiful shop. Thankfully, Southern Crossing has found a new home right around the corner on 8th Street in the heart of downtown Opelika.

Southern Crossing carries product lines that are unique to their store and not found in other retail locations in Opelika. Mud Pie, enewton design jewelry, Capri Blue Candles, Nora Fleming, and more contribute items that make this gift shop very special. The store specializes in gifts for all ages and all occasions, with bridal and baby registries being extremely popular. Something else that sets Southern Crossing apart is their beautiful, complimentary gift wrapping. The gorgeous bows are works of art.

Someone who receives a gift from Southern Crossing is likely to spend extra time admiring the way it looks before they open it.

108 S 8th St., Opelika, 334-703-3273
southerncrossingopelika.com

95

SEE THE RESULTS OF A MOTHER-DAUGHTER EFFORT

AT FIG & WASP IN WAVERLY

Owners Meredith Frye and her mother Scout make a great team in their little shop in Waverly, Alabama. Scout does pottery, and Meredith paints. The pottery has a distinctive look consisting primarily of white pieces with a warm white glaze. Just as the fig and the fig wasp need each other in a cozy, symbiotic, mutually dependent relationship, so do Scout and Meredith need each other as they work in the store and search for treasures, such as antiques from Europe, to bring home for their customers. The store specializes in French and English antiques.

Meredith contributes to her children's school by teaching art, and many of the paintings on display are her original works. Scout's coffee mugs and cheese and cracker trays are some of the store's best-selling items. They also carry vintage rugs, decorative pillows, and estate jewelry. Painted ceramic guinea hens are especially eye-catching. Fig & Wasp has regular store hours Wednesday through Sunday, but it's only open by appointment on Monday and Tuesday.

1500 Patrick St., Waverly, 334-444-0241
figandwasp.com

BUY GIFTS WITH MEANING

AT WRAPSODY IN DOWNTOWN AUBURN

The building housing Wrapsody, a popular gift boutique on North College Street, steps away from Toomer's Corner, has been holding court in that coveted location since 1892 when it began its life as a restaurant with a Greek owner. Later it was a soda shop, and if you look closely, you can still see the marks from the stools where customers sipped their root beer floats.

Owner Christie Howell has made Wrapsody the go-to spot for Greek-themed items that serve the sororities on campus, and you'll find jewelry, candles, kitchen and drinkware, gourmet foods, handbags, clothing, shoes, stationery, and more. Two notable brands carried inside Wrapsody are Able and Ronaldo. Able is focused on employing women who are coming out of difficult situations, such as prostitution, addiction, or poverty. Their leather goods are made in Africa, but the jewelry comes from Nashville. Ronaldo products are made in the US, and all their bracelets have special meanings that enhance their beauty.

112 N College St., 334-887-7447
wrapsodyonline.com

97

MEET FRIENDS AND READ A GREAT BOOK AT AUBURN OIL CO. BOOKSELLERS

Auburn Oil Co. Booksellers is an independent, family-owned bookstore, but it is also a comfortable gathering place. College students as well as Auburn residents enjoy walking in, ordering a specialty coffee, and then finding a spot to study or enjoy conversation with a friend.

Auburn Oil Co. Bookstore hosts book clubs, story time for children on Tuesdays and Saturdays, author conversations, teacher happy hours, and wine pairings. During those pairings, six wines are paired with six books, and for $30 you get a tasting of all six and a choice of one of the books.

The signature drinks served at the coffee bar have names inspired by authors or books. Some of them are Ace Detective, Rick Bragg, Jekyll/Hyde, The Gatsby, Pollyanna, and more. Sweet treats come from Camilla Kitchen and include cookies, muffins, and oatmeal energy bites. Auburn Oil Co. Booksellers is in the section of Magnolia Avenue between Toomer's Drugs and the Irritable Bao.

149 E Magnolia Ave., Ste. A, 334-246-3003
auburnoilbooksellers.com

CREATE A SIGNATURE SCENT
AT AUBURN CANDLE COMPANY

Who would guess that a candle company would make a great date (or friend) night activity? At Auburn Candle Company, you can come in and pour your own candle on the spot, complete with your preferred signature scent. Truthfully, this is a great Valentine's Day activity. Imagine choosing from over 85 fragrances and a wide variety of glass and ceramic vessels. Candle pouring takes about an hour, and reservations through the website are strongly recommended.

If you need a special gift and don't have time to make it yourself, plenty of made-in-house products are readily available. In addition to candles, you can choose wax melts, reed diffusers, and room sprays. Enticing fragrances include Cranberry Apple Marmalade, Cinnamon Buns, and Pink Sugar Balsam Fir in the winter to Coastal Linen, Sunflower, and Lavender in the summer, with dozens more in between.

Auburn Candle Company is in a beautiful converted home and is open seven days a week.

166 N Gay St., 334-209-2955
auburncandle.com

FIND THE PERFECT SLOUCHY AND MORE
AT THE MINT JULEP BOUTIQUE

The Mint Julep Boutique has been a fixture in Auburn for 10 years and in its present location for five. The brick-and-mortar store is in the Auburn Mall, but many customers shop Mint Julep products online. The warehouse is also located in Auburn. As an added perk for shoppers in Auburn, they can contact a store employee about a particular item and then go to the store to try it on and see it in person before buying it. When they arrive, clients will see attractive accessories that are only available inside the store.

Mint Julep carries primarily small, medium, and large sizes for women that are said to be generously proportioned. The store is known for its baggy sweater style known as "The Slouchy." Followers know to watch for "Slouchy Sundays," when those sweaters are sold at a discounted price.

Merchandise is attractively displayed and focuses on the seasons. Several items are heavily sequined to catch attention with plenty of bling.

1627 Opelika Rd., 334-246-3621
shopthemint.com

Another store near the Auburn Mall that you will want to check out is Home + Vine, which sells apparel, accessories, gifts, and home décor. The store is owned by Tori Brinson, and it is in the Gatewood Plaza.

1212 Gatewood Dr., Ste. A-1, 334-521-7485
homeandvineauburn.com

100

BUY AN AUBIE COOKIE OR AN ARCHITECTURALLY STUNNING CAKE

AT CAKEITECTURE

A favorite bakery in downtown Opelika is Cakeitecture. Carie Tindill is the owner and chief creator, and her cakes reflect imagination and a keen knowledge of architecture. There is a good reason for that. Tindill earned a Bachelor of Architecture degree from Auburn and a master's degree in integrated design and construction. After working in that field for several years, she decided to turn to her love for cooking and baking. She now uses the skills and tools of architecture as she designs and bakes stunning cakes.

In addition to cakes, Tindill's bakery is the licensed producer of the Aubie cookies infused with Toomer's Lemonade that are sold at Toomer's Drugs in downtown Auburn. She has other iced cookie designs for sale in Opelika, as well as cupcakes, cake pops, brownies, bars, and more.

Lee Dow, Tindill's administrative specialist, brings her own cooking skills to the business as well as a degree in art and interior design. They make a great creative team.

124 S 8th St., Opelika, 334-246-3002
cakeitecture.com

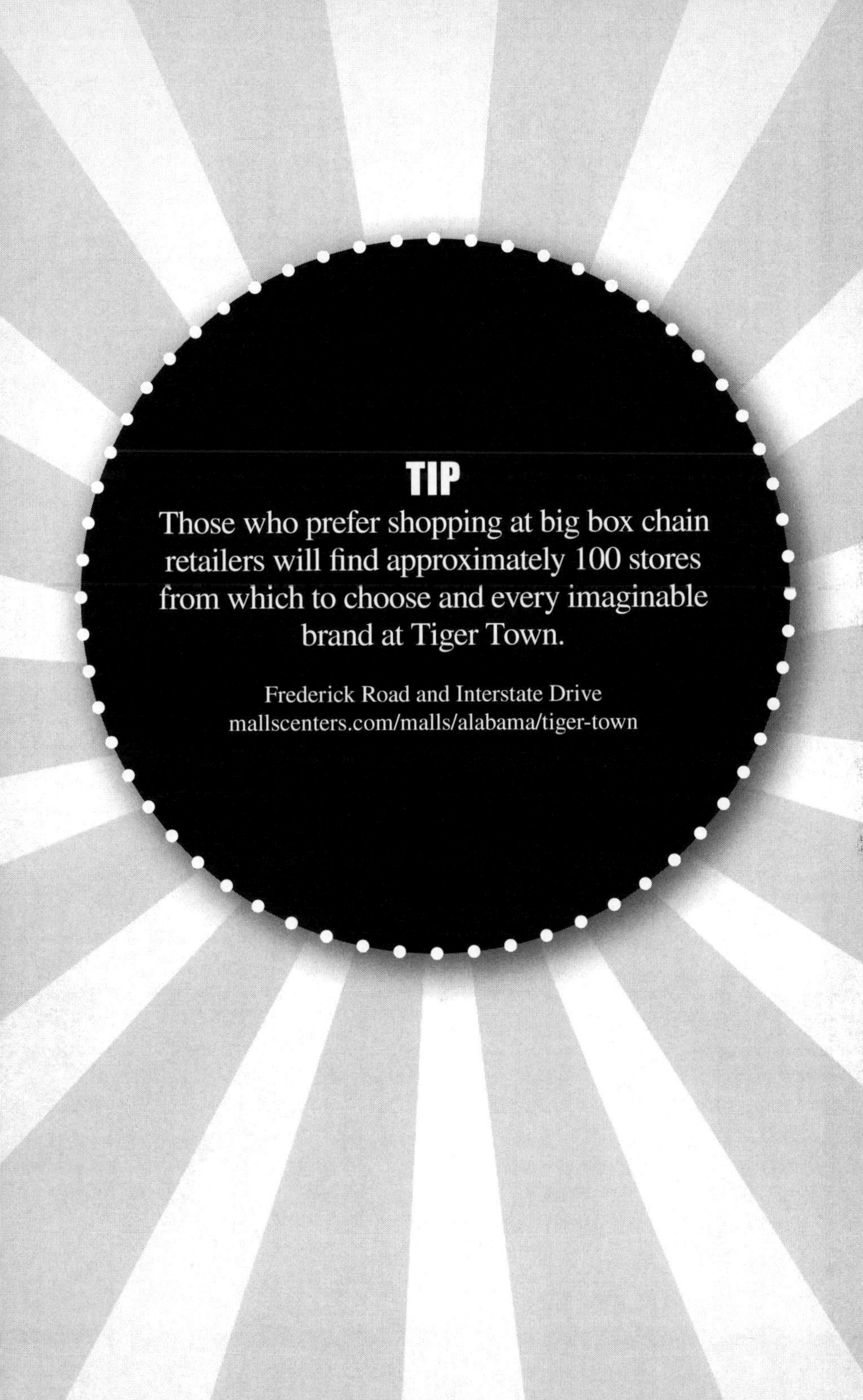
TIP
Those who prefer shopping at big box chain retailers will find approximately 100 stores from which to choose and every imaginable brand at Tiger Town.
Frederick Road and Interstate Drive
mallscenters.com/malls/alabama/tiger-town

Bow & Arrow, restaurant
owned by David Bancroft

ACTIVITIES
BY SEASON

SPRING

Hit the Target at Tumble Tree Disc Golf, 74

Support a Great Cause by Biking in Bo Bikes Bama, 91

Watch the Bull Riders or Dance to the Music at Auburn Rodeo, 50

Find the 11 Public Murals in Auburn and Opelika, 104

Catch Beads at the Mardi Gras Parade in Downtown Auburn, 64

Head to Kiesel Park in the Spring for Auburn CityFest, 67

Tour the Jule Collins Smith Museum of Fine Art, 102

Drive the Auburn Floral Trail in the Spring, 81

Catch a Homerun Ball at Plainsman Park (Samford Stadium-Hitchcock Field), 88

Listen to Country Music at Old 280 Boogie at Standard Deluxe in Waverly, 56

Request a Spot on the Patio at LiveOaks, 38

Watch Auburn Theatre Students Perform at the Telfair B. Peet Theatre, 101

SUMMER

Cast Your Rod and Catch Your Supper at Lee County Public Fishing Lake, 82

Learn to Play a Popular New Sport at the Opelika Pickleball Facility, 75

Recall Great Auburn Athletes as You Walk the Tiger Trail, 98

Grab Some Friends and Head to Tigertown Sports, 79

Bring Your Binoculars to One of the Piedmont Plateau Birding Trails, 76

Refresh with Lemonade at Toomer's Drugs, 14
Sink a Putt at Grand National Golf Course in Opelika, 80
Improve your Backhand at Yarbrough Tennis Center, 83
Find a Spot at Monkey Park for the Summer Swing Concert Series, 66
Test Your Inner Daredevil Skills at the New Auburn-Opelika Skate Park, 89

FALL

Watch for Ghosts at Salem-Shotwell Covered Bridge, 97
Discover a Rising Star at the Opelika Songwriters Festival and the Sound Wall, 47
Find Original Crafts at Syrup Soppin' Day in Pioneer Park at Loachapoka, 58
Watch the Eagle Soar at Jordan-Hare Stadium, 84
Join the Crowd for Oktoberfest at Ag Heritage Park, 48
Get a Closeup Look at Raptors during "Football, Fans, and Feathers," 51
Meet Friends and Read a Great Book at Auburn Oil Co. Booksellers, 130
Pitch a Tent for Tailgating before Home Football Games, 52
Listen to Country Music at Old 280 Boogie at Standard Deluxe in Waverly, 56
Go Mountain Biking or Camping at Chewacla State Park, 72
Join the Throng for Tiger Walk before Home Football Games, 86
Roll Toomer's Corner after a Big Auburn Victory, 90
Sample, Shop, and Listen at On the Tracks—A Wine and Cheese Event, 49
Buy Everything Orange and Blue at the Auburn University Bookstore, 116
Carry On a Long-Standing Tradition by Visiting J & M Bookstore, 120

WINTER

Admire the Gingerbread Village Inside The Hotel at Auburn University, 60

Step Back in Time at a Victorian Front Porch Christmas Tour, 62

Create a Signature Scent at Auburn Candle Company, 131

Peek Inside Beautiful Buildings at the Loveliest Village Christmas Tour, 57

Solve the Mysteries at Auburn Escape Zones, 71

Gather, Read, and Sample Treats at Well-Red Coffee, Books & Wine, 123

Escape the Rain and Cold with Indoor Fun at Good Times Bowling, 77

Be Dazzled by the Talent at the Jay and Susie Gogue Performing Arts Center, 46

Add Your Rumble to the Jungle at Neville Arena, 85

Take a Class and See Works by Local Artists at Art Haus, 108

Spend Hours Searching for Treasures at Angel's Antique & Flea Mall, 115

SUGGESTED ITINERARIES

FOR MUSEUM LOVERS

Marvel at Intricate Specimens Inside the Museum of Natural History, 100

Be Surprised at the Museum of Wonder in Seale, 105

Learn Surprising History at the Museum of East Alabama, 96

Tour the Jule Collins Smith Museum of Fine Art, 102

Dig Deeper into African American History at Nearby Tuskegee University, 106

DATE NIGHT

Buy a Ticket for a Performance at the Opelika Center for the Performing Arts, 54

Discover Amsterdam Café, A Gem on Gay Street, 3

Experience World-Class Service and Cuisine at 1856 Culinary Residence, 6

Come As You Are for Lunch or Dinner at Hamilton's on Magnolia, 9

Imagine Scenes from the 1800s during a Fine Meal at the Depot, 10

Watch Auburn Theatre Students Perform at the Telfair B. Peet Theatre, 101

Admire the Furnishings While You Eat a Great Meal at the Hound, 12

Take Your Own Good Vibes into Lucy's, 15

Have an Authentic Italian Meal at Ariccia Cucina, 4

Create a Signature Scent at Auburn Candle Company, 131

Taste Why Chef David Bancroft Is One of the South's Best by Dining at Acre, 2

Feast on Gulf Seafood, Wild Game, and More at Vintage 2298, 17

Shop, Stroll the Grounds, and Dine at Botanic, 18

Make the Drive to Find a Slower Pace and Great Food at rhe Waverly Local, 21

Be Transported to Ireland at Irish Bred Pub, 39

Devour a Great Steak or Fresh Oysters at Big Mike's Steakhouse, 26

Dine Sumptuously in Vintage Surroundings at Zazu Gastropub, 28

Request a Spot on the Patio at LiveOaks, 38

Make a Special Occasion Even More Delightful at Café 123, 8

Be Dazzled by the Talent at the Jay and Susie Gogue Performing Arts Center, 46

FREE ENTERTAINMENT

Learn Surprising History at the Museum of East Alabama, 96

Drive the Auburn Floral Trail in the Spring, 81

Roll Toomer's Corner after a Big Auburn Victory, 90

Find the 11 Public Murals in Auburn and Opelika, 104

Watch for Ghosts at Salem-Shotwell Covered Bridge, 97

Join the Throng for Tiger Walk before Home Football Games, 86

Surround Yourself with Nature at Kreher Preserve and Nature Center, 70

Recall Great Auburn Athletes as You Walk the Tiger Trail, 98

THE GREAT OUTDOORS

Support a Great Cause by Biking in Bo Bikes Bama, 91

Go Mountain Biking or Camping at Chewacla State Park, 72

Cast your Rod and Catch your Supper at Lee County Public Fishing Lake, 82

Bring Your Binoculars to One of the Piedmont Plateau Birding Trails, 76

Sink a Putt at Grand National Golf Course in Opelika, 80

Zipline Across the Alabama/Georgia State Line, 92

Surround Yourself with Nature at Kreher Preserve and Nature Center, 70

FAMILY FUN

Pitch a Tent for Tailgating before Home Football Games, 52

Head to Kiesel Park in the Spring for Auburn CityFest, 67

Find Original Crafts at Syrup Soppin' Day at Pioneer Park in Loachapoka, 58

Admire the Gingerbread Village inside The Hotel at Auburn University, 60

Join the Crowd for Oktoberfest at Ag Heritage Park, 48

Catch Beads at the Mardi Gras Parade in Downtown Auburn, 64

Get a Closeup Look at Raptors during "Football, Fans, and Feathers," 51

Find a Spot at Monkey Park for the Summer Swing Concert Series, 66

INDEX

10,000 Hz Records, 114
1856 Culinary Residence, 6
Acre, 2
Ag Heritage Park, 48
Agricultural & Mechanical College of Alabama, 121
Alabama Birding Trail, 76, 82
Alabama Polytechnic Institute, 121
Amsterdam Café, 3
Angel's Antique & Flea Mall, 115
Anthony, Butch, 105
Ariccia Cucina, 4
Art Haus, 108, 109
Artifactory, 118
Auburn Art, 119
Auburn Beautification Council, 81
Auburn Candle Company, 131
Auburn CityFest, 67
Auburn Creed, xii
Auburn Escape Zones, 71
Auburn Floral Trail, 81
Auburn IMG Sports Network, 53
Auburn Oil Co. Booksellers, 130
Auburn Preservation League, 57
Auburn Rodeo, 50
Auburn University, 2, 5, 11, 32, 35, 52, 57, 60, 83, 84, 96, 98, 100, 108, 110, 111, 116, 118, 119, 121
Auburn University Bookstore, 116
Auburn University Museum of Natural History, 100
Auburn University School of Veterinary Medicine, 51, 87
Bancroft, Chef David, 2, 30
Barkley, Charles, 99
Bean Coffee Shop, 33
Beasecker, Keely, 20
Behind the Glass, 124
Big Blue Bagel & Deli, 33
Big Mike's Steakhouse, 26
Blue Heron Adventure Park, 92
Bo Bikes Bama, 91
Botanic, 18
Bow & Arrow, 30
Brown, Stacy, 18, 19
Buc-ee's, 117
Burcham, Andy, 53
Byron's Smokehouse, 31
Café 123, 8
Cakeitecture, 134
Campbell, Jason, 53

Central Alabama Mountain Peddlers, 72
Chattahoochee River 92, 93
Cheeto's, 37
Chewacla State Park, 72, 76
Chickchickporkpork, 37
Chicken Salad Chick, 19
Chuck's Bar-B-Que, 27
City Mills Hotel, 93
Coffee Cat, 13
Collegiate Hotel, 65
Country's Barbecue, 24
Dam Food Truck, 3
Dam Taco Truck, 3
Depot, 10, 11
Dough Pizzeria, 29
Draughon, Caroline Marshall, 110, 111
Draughon, Ralph Brown, 5
Drive-Thru Museum, 105
Dye, Coach Pat, 34
Dykes, Whitley, 16
East Alabama Male College, 110, 121
E. W. Shell Fisheries Center, 11
Fig & Wasp, 128
Food Truck Fridays, 42
Food Truck Saturdays, 42
Football, Fans, and Feathers, 51
Gallagher, Chef Pat, 9
Gallery on Railroad, 125
George Washington Carver Museum, 106
Gingerbread Village, 57, 60
Good Times Bowling, 77
Gourmet Tigers, 61
Grand National Golf Course, 80
Green Monster, 88
Guthrie's, 23
Haley Center, 116
Hamilton's on Magnolia, 9, 124
Hare, Cliff, 84, 99
Heritage House Inn, 62, 63
Hey Day Market, 35
Home + Vine, 133
Honey Badger Bakery, 61
Hotel at Auburn University, 5, 35, 57, 60
Hound, 12, 13
Hudson, Tim, 88
Irish Bred Pub, 39
Iron Bowl, 38, 84
Irritable Bao, 16, 130
J & M Bookstore, 104, 120
Jackson, Bo, 34, 88, 91, 99
Jay and Susie Gogue Performing Arts Center, 46
Jordan, Shug, 98
Jordan-Hare Stadium, 22, 52, 60, 84, 86, 116

Jule Collins Smith Museum of Fine Art, 102, 103
Kiesel Park, 67, 73
Kreher Preserve and Nature Center, 70
Lake Martin, 20, 82
Laurel Hotel and Spa, 7
Lee County Historical Society Museum, 58
Lee County Public Fishing Lake, 76, 82
Legacy Museum, 106
Lemonade, 14, 119, 134
LiveOaks, 38
Loachapoka, 58, 59
Loveliest Village Christmas Tour, 57
Lucy's, 15, 52
Magnolia James Boutique, 118
Mardi Gras Parade, 64
Mint Julep Boutique, 132
Mo'Bay Beignet Co., 32
Momma Goldberg's Deli, 22
Monkey Park, 66
Mrs. Story's Dairy Bar, 25
Murals, 96, 104
Museum of East Alabama, 96, 104
Museum of Wonder, 105
National Infantry Museum, 93
Neville Arena, 85
Newton, Cam, 34, 99
Nicolaisen, Chef Robbie, 12
Niffer's Place, 20
Norma Rae, 96
Nunn-Winston House, 67
Oaks, 106
O Grows, 43
Oktoberfest, 48
Old 280 Boogie at Standard Deluxe, 56
Olson, Gregg, 88
On The Tracks, 49
One Bike Coffee, 33
Opelika Center for the Performing Arts, 54
Opelika Community Archery Park, 78
Opelika High School, 49, 54, 66
Opelika Pickleball Facility, 75
Opelika Songwriters Festival, 47
Osher Lifelong Learning Institute, 111
Pannie-George's Kitchen, 34
Paolina, Chef Brian, 15
Pebble Hill, 110
Petrie, George, xii
Pickleball, 75
Piedmont Plateau Birding Trails, 76
Pioneer Park, 58
Plainsman Park, 88
Rooftop Terrace, 6

Ross House Coffee, 33
Salem-Shotwell Covered Bridge, 97
Sheila C's Burger Barn, 42
Slocumb, Rob and Jen, 47
Smith, Albert J. Jr., 103
SNF Outdoor Products, 13
Sound Wall, 47
Southeastern Raptor Center, 51, 67
Southern Crossing, 127
Southern Union State Community College, 54
Spring Villa, 78
Stern, Henry J., 109
Stern, J. and Ginger, 108
Sullivan, Pat, 20, 99, 119
Summer Swing Concert Series, 66
Syrup Soppin' Day, 58
Tailgating, 52
Tart & Tartan, 61
Telfair B. Peet Theatre, 101
Thomas, Frank, 88, 99
Tigertown Sports, 79
Tiger Trail, 98
Tiger Walk, 86
Tony and Libba Rane Culinary Science Center, 6, 35
Toomer's Corner, 2, 5, 38, 60, 81, 90, 98, 119, 129
Toomer's Drugs, 14, 130, 134
Tuberville, Tommy, 34
Tumble Tree Disc Golf, 74
Tuskegee Airmen National Historic Site, 106
Tuskegee Institute National Historic Site, 106
Tuskegee University, 106
Venditori's, 40
Victorian Front Porch Christmas Tour, 57, 62, 63
Wakefield Home, 126
Walk-On's Sports Bistreaux, 41
Ware Jewelers, 121, 122
Watason, Chef Christian, 21
Waverly Local, 21
Whitewater Express, 92
Wrapsody, 104, 129
Wreck Tech Pajama Parade, 10
Wright's Market, 43
Yarbrough Tennis Center, 83
Zazu Gastropub, 28, 29